Business Statistics
on the Web

Business
Statistics
on the Web

Find Them Fast—
At Little or No Cost

Paula Berinstein

CyberAge Books

Medford, New Jersey

Business Statistics on the Web:
Find Them Fast—At Little or No Cost

Library of Congress Cataloging-in-Publication Data

Berinstein, Paula.
    Business statistics on the web : find them fast-at little or no cost / Paula Berinstein.
        p. cm.
      ISBN: 0-910965-65-X
  1. Commercial statistics--Computer network resources. 2. United States--Statistics--Computer network resources. 3. Electronic information resource searching. I. Title.

    HF1016.B47 2003
    025.046'33--dc21

                                        2003007982

Printed and bound in the United States of America.

Publisher: Thomas H. Hogan, Sr.
Editor-in-Chief: John B. Bryans
Managing Editor: Deborah R. Poulson
Copy Editor: Pat Hadley-Miller
Proofreader: Kimberly Shigo
Graphics Department Director: M. Heide Dengler
Book Design: Kara Mia Jalkowski
Cover Design: Laura Hegyi
Indexer: Sharon Hughes

To John Bryans

Contents

Sidebars and Case Studies

Foreword

How many times have we offered or received the advice, "You must be able to find it on the Web?" The advice is correct and easy to dispense; finding the information can be much harder and take a lot of time, even with today's sophisticated search engines.

Searching for statistics and other information now occupies more user time than any other activity on the Web. People in business, government, charities, public service, research institutions, and schools spend an average of 60 minutes searching the Web per day.

In business, time is money, and having access to efficient strategies for finding important statistics saves time, saves money, and may just make or save the company or institution! While we depend on anecdotal information about our customers and competitors, we need objective, quantifiable ways to measure our aspirations, our chances of achieving our goals, our strategies, and our progress. How large is the market for our products? What will we have to pay to make those products, and how does that amount compare with standard costs for our industry? How do we stack up against our competitors? What is the outlook for the economy? What are the dynamics of our industry? Whether it is a business plan for a startup, a marketing plan for a successful company, economic analysis by government and think tanks, or company financials for competitor analysis, sound numbers are critical to our success.

To fully appreciate the importance of reliable statistics to a business, imagine what happens when we do without them. A startup that does not size its potential market accurately fails to win investment. A moderately successful company stumbles because it miscalculates demand. A mature company decides not to introduce a new product, and its biggest competitor steals the market.

Many organizations do without much of this valuable information, either because they fail to appreciate its significance, lack the staff to acquire and analyze it, or do not know where to locate it. They are sowing the seeds of their own failure. All that work invested in the creation and operation of a business, people's livelihoods at stake, and they fly by the seat of their pants. Great companies were never built that way.

Admittedly, until recently it has been extremely difficult to come by many types of business statistics. Before the Internet, even regularly published government economic and financial publications could be elusive, residing primarily in libraries, where few businesspeople set foot. Even now, it has taken years for many businesses to get fast, reliable Internet access, and many still do not know about the availability of even basic statistical sources.

And what of market size, that most critical and elusive jewel? How many of us know how to find it? Do we know how to find detailed, current information on our industry and competition that doesn't cost an arm and a leg? Perhaps we type a few words into a search engine, but, overwhelmed by the tidal wave of results, most of us throw our hands up. Fewer of us think to call libraries, many of which offer quite good free services.

If you have purchased this book, it is because you want to correct this situation, and that is exactly what Paula Berinstein will help you do. An experienced researcher with 25 years of experience, she has learned the good, old-fashioned way, through trial and error, how to find statistics on a tight budget. So good is she at this pursuit that she has made a name for herself as a specialist in statistics, not a common area of focus among business researchers.

This volume is a compilation of Berinstein's current wisdom on the subject of finding and estimating business statistics. In appreciation of your budget, she offers sources that almost without exception are available at little or no cost, or at least met that criterion at publication time. As always with Berinstein's books, there is a useful Quick Start section that distills the best tips and resources to get you going fast. Following that brief chapter, the book is divided into four basic sections: a statistics primer that covers who publishes statistics and what to look for in using them; basic search techniques; Web-based resources covering markets, industries, economics, finance, company financials, and general business for most of the English-speaking world and portions of the rest of it; and special tips and tricks, including methods for estimating company financials. Berinstein's previous book in this area, *Finding Statistics Online*, emphasized American sources, but, having recently wed one of my countrymen, she has realized that businesspeople in the rest of the world will also benefit from her expertise.

You will find her case studies enlightening. In them, Berinstein shares her thinking as she meets and sidesteps obstacles. The search process is not always smooth sailing, but you can navigate your way around the hazards and false dead ends if you apply her techniques. Her case studies also illustrate the breadth and depth of information you can find on the Web—information that used to require the expertise of dedicated searchers using expensive databases and arcane library sources to ferret out.

Perhaps the greatest benefit you will take away from this book is the ability to examine your problem methodically and formulate sound search strategies. Yes, it is important to be familiar with the various trade magazines, government organizations, associations, universities, companies, and think tanks that produce the information. However, it is even more important to know how to identify them. This skill Berinstein teaches well, for she believes that it is more important to teach people how to fish than simply to put a ready-cooked meal in front of them.

You don't have to be intimidated by statistics. With a copy of *Business Statistics on the Web* next to your keyboard, you will be fortified for the search that might just make your fortune or save your business. What are you waiting for?

Charles Cotton
Former Executive Chairman, GlobespanVirata
Cambridge, England

Acknowledgments

Every book is a collaborative work inspired, fueled, and nurtured by numerous people besides the author. And so I would like to thank the following wonderful friends and colleagues for their help and support ...

All the fine people at Information Today, Inc., including:

My editor John Bryans

Deborah Poulson, managing editor

Kara Mia Jalkowski, who designed the book

Laura Hegyi, who created the cover

Lisa Wrigley, book marketing coordinator

Also:

Darrell Huff, seminal statistics book author

Charles Cotton, for his superb foreword

Clay Helberg, whose review of *Finding Statistics Online* in *The American Statistician* provided useful suggestions, most of which I have incorporated into this book

Alan Jones, for his help with statistics basics

Gina Giamanco at Factiva

My friends Kathy and Scott, Gary and Barb, Jim, Howard, Karen, Barbara, Marina, Mark and Susan, Greg and Linda, John and Crystal, Mark M., Pat and Tom, the other Tom and Bev, Alan and Claire, Steve and Lisa, Barry and Michael, Ken W., Trung, Jules, Andy from Cambridge, and Greg Q.

My parents

My sister Jan

My in-laws, Eileen and Gerry, Louise and Graham

My fabulous stepkids, Ellie and Alex

About the Web Page

My Web site at http://www.berinsteinresesarch.com offers a wealth of business statistics links for your convenience. The site contains links not present in the book and vice versa, so, to derive maximum benefit, be sure to consult both.

The online resources are listed under the same subject headings used in the book. In some cases, items are listed under more than one heading, as they are here. Most of the links are arranged geographically so that you can zero in quickly on resources for the country or region you're researching.

Please let me know if you have found a link I should add to my site. I would also appreciate your help in identifying links that do not work. You can reach me at pberinstein@att.net.

Preface

Much has changed since *Finding Statistics Online* was published in 1998. Back in those days, information professionals possessed a towering advantage over casual searchers when it came to finding statistics using online systems. In the time since then, that edge has narrowed significantly. Today anyone with basic Web skills can find statistics, or at least come up with promising leads to offline information.

Two developments are responsible for this change: the appearance of the Google search engine and reasonably priced pay-as-you-go search services on the Web. No longer do you have to subscribe to expensive and difficult-to-use information systems of the kind found in libraries. Sure, those still work. They are still as powerful as ever and completely appropriate for dedicated searchers. But they are no longer the only game in town.

Yes, statistics are still elusive, and yes, the more specific the request the more difficult to fulfill it, but the path to useful tidbits is far shorter than it used to be. For that reason, my tip list is shorter than in *Finding Statistics Online*, with the specific resources more focused and numerous. My goal for this book is to get you in and out quickly, with useful information in your possession by the time you leave the Web.

Who Should Read This Book

Business Statistics on the Web is aimed at businesspeople, journalists, public relations specialists, students, teachers, researchers, and anyone else wishing to find statistics about business and economics.

You will find this book useful if you need numbers for:

- Decision-making

- Business plans

- Press releases

- Speeches

- Proposals

- Presentations and interviews

- Course work, theses, and dissertations

- White papers

- Books, articles, and editorials

- Learning about a topic

- Understanding your competition and your customers

- Assessing opportunities

- Marketing and advertising strategy

- Job hunting and recruiting

and more.

What's in This Book

Business Statistics on the Web enables you to find:

- Market size

- Market share

- Company financial information

- Units sold

- Economic and business indicators

- Demographics

- Cost of labor

- Prices

- Consumer attitudes and trends

- Securities information

- National accounts

and much, much more.

There are many more short case studies in this book than in its predecessor. These boxed blurbs are designed to help you shape your strategy and to illustrate the types of information you can find easily. I have also included some extensive case studies that illustrate the difficulties you can encounter when searching and that offer solutions for surmounting them. In these longer examples, I have attempted to convey how I think problems through rather than simply show you the neat final answer. Believe me, experienced searchers hit snags, too. Sometimes we can't find the answer at all!

To deal with this problem, the book offers a special new feature: a chapter on techniques for estimating numbers you can't get. Read it and you will not simply tax your little grey cells, you will also find yourself ahead of those who throw up their hands when they can't find exact numbers.

Business Statistics on the Web offers a wider range of geographic coverage than did *Finding Statistics Online*. (One learns from life and from reviews.) Though you will find resources from around the world mentioned here, I have emphasized those from the following English-speaking countries: the U.S., Canada, the United Kingdom, Ireland, Australia, and New Zealand.

I have not included specific databases from library-type systems like LexisNexis, DIALOG, DataStar, etc. in this book because of the audience to which it is addressed. If you want to use those systems, refer to my lists in *Finding Statistics Online* as well as the system documentation. The search techniques I outlined in *Finding Statistics Online* still work, and many, though not all, resources are the same.

My standards for Web site inclusions are usefulness, usability, and price. Most of the sites in this book are free. I personally looked at every one. It's pretty much true that if a site doesn't offer statistics, is expensive, or doesn't publish its prices, it didn't make it into the book. I offer a few exceptions. Some of the sites I included are open both to subscribers/members and nonsubscribers/nonmembers. Obviously, if you're a member, you get more information, but you don't have to be one. Some sites offer free information, and some offer low-cost information. Others provide a mix of the two options. Sites open only to members didn't make the grade. However, if you happen upon one of these closed sites, don't automatically discount it. Call or e-mail and see what the proprietors offer for a price. Sometimes associations will even give out free information if you don't need much.

Sources that charge are indicated with a dollar sign, $, at the end of the listing. Do not assume that everything on such a site costs money, however. In some cases I have mentioned that the site also offers free material, but because charging policies and offerings change so rapidly, you ought to take a look for yourself.

I have annotated many of the listings. Where the name of the resource makes the content self-explanatory, I have often omitted the annotation. In certain cases I left annotations off because the site content is likely to change often, and I did not want to mislead.

Here is the basic organization of the book:

Chapter 1: Quick Start. This breezy chapter offers the best tips and starting points for busy people.

Chapter 2: Statistics Basics. This statistics primer is a reprise of the one in *Finding Statistics Online*, with some changes.

Chapter 3: Who Generates and Publishes Statistics? You should have an idea of the types of organizations that create and publish statistics so you'll be able to make educated guesses about where to find them. This chapter also offers Web-based resources for identifying trade associations and journals and government agencies.

Chapter 4: General Search Tips. This chapter expands on the quick start outlined in Chapter 1.

Chapter 5: U.S. Industry Sources. Here I offer the best resources for investigating U.S. industries.

Chapter 6: Non-U.S. Industry Sources. This chapter is much like Chapter 5, but it covers Australia, Canada, Ireland, New Zealand, and the U.K. in detail, Europe and the world to some degree, and other countries at a basic level. Just so you'll know, I focused on the above areas because of my lack of expertise in most foreign languages, not because I suffer from myopia. I suggest to my fellow more-fluent authors that companion books covering the rest of the world in depth might be well received. (Okay, I probably could have included Italy without help, but that would have made the book unpredictable, and I can hear the reviewers now!)

Chapter 7: Market Research Sources. This chapter is short and sweet. Though tiny, it stands on its own by virtue of its subject matter.

Chapter 8: Economic and Financial Statistics. This chapter includes sources for economic and financial statistics not present in the other chapters. It is by no means the only place in the book to find them. Look for them also in government sources: See the list of gateways in Chapter 3 and central banks and national agencies in Chapter 6.

Chapter 9: Company Information. What is business information without knowledge of the competition? You will find sources for your competitors' public information here. To discern their innermost secrets, consult Chapter 12, which shows you how to estimate what's going on behind closed doors.

Chapter 10: Demographics and Population Statistics. I can't describe the subject matter any better than that.

Chapter 11: Special Tips and Tricks. This chapter presents some of my ideas for particular types of sources and how to use them.

Chapter 12: Your Competitive Advantage: Estimating Company Numbers You Can't Get. It takes some work to figure out what's going on in private companies and in subsidiaries and divisions of public ones, but you can do it if you put your mind to it. And read this chapter.

Appendix: Glossary of Statistics Terms. This lexicon is largely the same as the one in *Finding Statistics Online*, with very minor changes.

Finally, be sure to consult my Web site at http://www.berinsteinresearch.com. The statistics metasite there includes some of the resources from this book as well as many you won't find here. Select "Statistics Links."

Chapter 1

Quick Start

This chapter cuts to the chase. Here are gathered the absolute best tips and sources for finding statistics on your topic. Try these first. Should they fail you, the rest of the book should not, especially if you use the back-of-the-book index to zoom in on your area of interest.

Sources
General

Your best general starting points for business statistics on the Web are:

Google, http://www.google.com. This fine general search engine has come out of nowhere to beat the others hands down. You can use it to zero in on specific phrases in Web documents. Google cannot see inside internal databases, however, so you may have to augment it with sources like Factiva and FindArticles, which search "official" article collections.

Factiva, http://www.factiva.com. Derived from Dow Jones Interactive and Reuters Business Briefing, Factiva.com offers a powerful search engine and impressive content. As an individual user, you pay very reasonable prices as you go. For $69 per year, you can search as much as you want and pay only for the content you select. The service offers nearly 8,000 publications from 118 countries and in 22 languages, including major news and business sources, trade journals, news wires, and general publications from around the world.

FindArticles, http://www.FindArticles.com. This free source for complete articles on a variety of topics is too good to be true.

BizJournals, http://www.bizjournals.com. This wonderful collection covers 41 local business journals from U.S. cities, and it's free!

Trade Journals

To identify trade journals, check the lists of journals covered by aggregators, such as:

Dialog, http://www.dialog.com. Go into the database catalog (select Sources, then Dialog and Dialog DataStar, then Dialog Database Catalog). You want the section on Search Aids and Source Lists, which starts on page 310 of the 2002 catalog. The list of 7,000 sources is voluminous, comprehensive, and alphabetically arranged, but you can search the PDF file by keywords and/or glance through it quickly. You don't have to be a subscriber to view this information.

Factiva, http://www.factiva.com. Select Products, then Dow Jones Interactive, then Article Archive. Then click on "Search the Publications Library source list."

FindArticles, http://www.FindArticles.com. Drill down by subject.

ProQuest, http://www.proquest.com. Under Products, select Business. You can choose from a variety of databases. Click on "More Product Information," then look for the title lists.

Or, you can consult directories like:

Google, http://www.google.com. Click on the Directory tab, then Business, News and Publications, Magazines. From there you can select Trade or look at the individual listings, which cover a variety of countries. You can also start with Regional at the top level and follow the same strategy to get to countries and regions around the world.

Yahoo!, http://www.yahoo.com. Go to Business and Economy, then News and Media. Select Magazines, then Trade Magazines, then the category in which you are interested. Consult the Yahoo! sites for various countries by selecting Regional from the top level menu, then following the same strategy.

Trade Associations

To identify associations online, consult the following sites.

United States

American Society of Association Executives, http://www.asaenet. org/main. Select the gateway to associations.

Associations on the Net from the Internet Public Library, http://ipl. sils.umich.edu/ref/AON

Directory of Associations from Business Know-How, http://www. businessknowhow.com/associations/search_associations.asp

Directory of Associations from Concept Marketing Group, Inc., http://www.marketingsource.com/associations. Lists more than 34,000 associations around the world. Searching and basic information are free. Detailed information requires a subscription. $

Google, http://directory.google.com/Top/Business/Resources/Associations. Google lists associations under a variety of categories. The URL here leads to business-related associations.

The Virtual Community of Associations, http://www.vcanet.org/vca/ assns.htm. Associations located in the greater Washington, DC area.

Yahoo! Trade Associations, http://dir.yahoo.com/Business_and_ Economy/Organizations/Trade_Associations. Multinational.

Australia and New Zealand

Business Organisations from PIPERS New Zealand Pages, http://www.piperpat.co.nz/nz/business/organs.html

Government and Business Associations Directory, Australia, http://www.business.gov.au

New Zealand Associations from BizInfo, http://www.bizinfo.co.nz

Yahoo! Australia and New Zealand, http://au.dir.yahoo.com/business _and_ economy/organisations/Trade_Associations

Canada

Associations Canada, http://circ.micromedia.ca

Canadian Associations from the Quebec Association of Export Trading Houses, http://www.amceq.org/Tools/en_association.htm

Hillwatch Directory of Associations, Interest groups, NGOs, Coalitions, and Corporations, http://www.hillwatch.com/lobbylist/LobbyHome.htm. Canadian and world information.

Yahoo! Canada, http://ca.dir.yahoo.com/business_and_economy/organizations/Trade_Associations

Ireland

Yahoo! U.K. and Ireland, http://uk.dir.yahoo.com/business_and _economy/organisations/trade_associations

U.K. and Northern Ireland

Directory of U.K. Trade Associations, http://www.brainstorm.co.uk/TANC/Directory/Welcome.html

Yahoo! U.K. and Ireland, http://uk.dir.yahoo.com/business_and_economy/organisations/trade_associations

Europe

Yahoo! European Organizations, http://dir.yahoo.com/Regional/ Regions/Europe/Business_and_Economy /Organizations

Yahoo! Regions, http://dir.yahoo.com/Regional/Regions. See individual regions and countries, Business and Economy, then Organizations.

You can also conduct a Google search using keywords you think should be in the association's name plus words like "association," "society," and "federation."

Government Gateways

These gateways will lead you to national government statistics, and in many cases, state, province, territory, and local ones as well.

United States

FedStats, http://www.fedstats.gov. A gateway to statistics offered by U.S. government agencies.

FirstGov, http://www.firstgov.gov. Gateway to the U.S. Federal government.

U.S. State Data Centers, http://www.census.gov/sdc/www

Australia and New Zealand

Australian Bureau of Statistics, http://www.abs.gov.au/Ausstats/abs @.nsf/ausstatshome

Australian Commonwealth Government Information, http://www. fed.gov.au/KSP. Includes links to both commonwealth and state/ territory Web sites.

New Zealand Government Online, http://www.govt.nz. Includes links to both Government of New Zealand and local government sites.

Statistics New Zealand, http://www.stats.govt.nz

Canada

Government of Canada, http://canada.gc.ca. Includes links to both national and provincial/territory governments.

Statistics Canada, http://www.statcan.ca

Ireland

Central Statistics Office Ireland, http://www.cso.ie

Government of Ireland, http://www.irlgov.ie. Includes links to both state agencies and local authorities.

United Kingdom and Northern Ireland

The Government of Northern Ireland, http://www.nics.gov.uk

Northern Ireland Statistics and Research Agency (NISRA), http://www.nisra.gov.uk. Official Northern Ireland statistics.

U.K. Government Online, http://www.ukonline.gov.uk. Includes links to federal and local agencies.

U.K. National Statistics Office, http://www.statistics.gov.uk

Europe

European Governments Online, http://europa.eu.int/abc/governments/index_en.html

The European Union, http://europa.eu.int

Search Tips

The two best tips for controlling your search are:

- Make sure you are searching for items in the current or previous year. You want your statistics to be as current as possible. (Of course, if you are looking for historical statistics, use the date or dates you prefer.)

- Search for phrases rather than individual words. This technique will help you zero in on the most relevant material and will eliminate most of the extraneous junk.

If the system you are using does not provide a way to limit by date, use the year you want as a search term. This technique, though not foolproof, will help eliminate older material.

Phrases are often designated by double quotes, as in *"business statistics."* Some systems indicate phrases differently, usually either by using a drop-down menu or by putting nothing but a single space between the words of a phrase, as in *business statistics*. You can combine phrases with single words or with each other, as in:

> *"aerospace industry" UK*
> *"handheld devices" "Palm OS"*

For specific information on how to do phrase and date searching, consult the hints in Chapter 4, General Search Tips, or the Help feature for the system you are using.

Chapter 2

Statistics Basics

When we hear the term *statistics*, most of us think of numbers associated with complicated analyses and dry-sounding terminology. Some people insist that statistics are all lies and should be ignored. Not many of us are clear about what statistics really are, how they come into being, and how to evaluate them. When we hear that "Fifty percent of Canadian Internet users have looked at online job postings" or "The median weekly earnings of men in the U.S. workforce are nearly a third higher than women's," we know what our emotional reaction is, but many of us don't think beyond that to examine whether the reaction is justified by the facts.

This chapter is a statistics primer. While it is the most technical chapter in the book, it will greatly help you select and defend some key numbers in your business or strategic plan, and it might make the difference between your securing funding and going begging. Read on, and you will learn what statistics are, how they are arrived at, and what to watch for when assessing their validity. The concepts and issues treated here will arise again and again in the case studies in this book and in your own searches: questions of definition, methodology, currency, and bias. Knowing what to look for doesn't mean that you have to read every word of every methodology discussion or contact every researcher whose data you're considering, though you may wish to do so. This chapter helps you develop a foundation for asking the right questions. You decide how far to go.

Types of Statistics

Statistics can take a variety of forms. Here are the types you'll encounter.

Raw Numbers. Raw numbers are pure data—they represent counts or measures. Population counts and company financials are examples of raw numbers. Sometimes raw numbers are reworked before release; you'll recognize such data by phrases like "adjusted for seasonal variations" or "in 1986 dollars." Counts of items that can only be measured in terms of specific values, such as people or cars or the number of books on a shelf, are said to represent *discrete data.* You cannot have 3.2 people or 1.75 cars or 26.2 books on a shelf. *Continuous data*, such as weights and heights, can be measured using any point along a continuum to describe their number. You can weigh 130.2 pounds or be 67.5 inches tall.

Percentages. Percentages express the relationships between a part and the whole and help make sense of raw data. Percentages are easy to work with because they reduce counts to one common scale, based on a hundred.

For example, if I say that American households spent an average of $1,903 for healthcare in 1998, $1,959 in 1999, and $2,066 in 2000, you can instantly recognize that people are spending more each year, but you can't tell how significant the differences are, particularly if you want to compare them to the rate of inflation. However, when you convert the numbers into percentages (up 2.9 percent in 1999, then another 5.5 percent from 1999 to 2000), you can appreciate the significance of the raw numbers.

However, percentages can overstate or understate the significance of the raw numbers, so they should be supplemented with a consideration of the actual data. How accurate a picture conveyed by percentages is depends on where you start and the nature of the thing being counted. For example, we often hear that there has been a large increase in this or that undesirable thing, and good grief, isn't that scary! Sometimes alarm is warranted, and sometimes not, depending on the actual numbers and what the thing is. If the price of a taco has jumped 43 percent from 35 cents to 50 cents, that 43 percent is less significant than if it represented the increase in the price of a car from $17,000 to more than $24,000. The next time you hear about percent increases or decreases in numbers of business failures, computer hackings, or bankruptcies, look for the raw numbers before you decide whether to be alarmed, relieved, or unimpressed.

Indexes. An index is a number that is computed to represent the value of a range of different items. Because an index expresses those items in terms of a common base, it enables us to compare apples to apples. An index may represent measurements or counts of many things, or different aspects of one thing. An example of the former is the consumer price index, which aggregates prices of many products and services. An example of the latter is gymnastic scoring, where many different attributes of gymnastic performance are being measured. An index may represent objective measurements such as prices, or subjective ones such as attitudes, feelings, and judgments.

Indexes are used as general indicators of the state of something. For example, the consumer price index says something about the state of the economy in general, as well as about prices of consumer goods. Familiar indexes include baseball player batting averages, Intelligence Quotient (IQ) scores, and crime rates.

Rankings. Ranking means placing something at various points on a scale or a list of sorted values. Two kinds of numbers are involved in ranking: the raw data and the rank or rating number. A searcher might seek the rank number, the raw data, or both.

For example, if you were to rank countries according to the amount of money they spend on foreign aid, you'd have to start with the actual amounts of money. That would be the raw data. Then, you'd rank the countries by amount, either the largest to the smallest, or vice versa. You'd have two numbers: the actual amount and the rank.

Rather than using the dollar amount, you might calculate the percent of the national budget represented by foreign aid. This process would require that you find two raw numbers: the amount spent on foreign aid and the total national budget. Note that because some countries have more money than others, a list based on percent of national budget would look different from a list based on raw numbers alone.

Averages. There are three common types of averages: mean, median, and mode. These are often different for any given group and they denote different things, so it's important to know which average is being used.

Mean. The mean is the arithmetic average of a group of numbers. The mean is arrived at by adding up all the values and dividing by the number of measurements. For example, the mean age in a family of four, with ages of 42, 40, 10, and 4, is 24 (the sum of the ages divided by four). Notice that the mean in this example does not reflect any real person's age. Means are what give us silly-sounding statements such as "The average family includes 2.3 children." Because it may result in hypothetical rather than real values, the mean can be an unattractive measure in certain situations.

The mean can be skewed so that it is less than representative of reality if it includes one or a few numbers at either the high or low extreme. Using the family example, the inclusion of a 90-year-old grandparent could raise the mean substantially to a little over 37; the addition of a one-year-old baby would affect the mean far less (without the grandparent, the mean would be 19.4 rather than 24). When you see a mean figure that doesn't look quite right, consider what and who might have been counted.

Median. The median is the midpoint of a group of numbers; half the numbers in the group fall above the median and half fall below the median. For example, the median home price in an area might be $250,000, with half the homes valued at less than $250,000 and half valued at more than $250,000. It could very well be, however, that there are no houses actually priced at $250,000 (just as there was no one in the family aged 24 in the mean example above).

The median tells nothing about the range or distribution of the data. We don't know the high and low extremes, and we don't know how many houses might sell around $180,000 as opposed to $60,000. The mean will probably be different for each of two or more neighborhoods with a median price of $250,000, depending on how the data are clustered.

Let's look at means and medians with a detailed example. Neighborhood A is structured as follows:

100 houses at	$120,000
10 houses at	$250,000
30 houses at	$260,000
30 houses at	$270,000
30 houses at	$280,000
5 houses at	$350,000
5 houses at	$400,000

Neighborhood A includes 210 houses. The median (midpoint) home price is $250,000: 10 homes cost $250,000, 100 homes cost less than $250,000, and 100 homes cost more than $250,000. Neighborhood A features a mean home price of $212,750. This number was computed by adding the price of each of the 210 houses and dividing by 210.

Neighborhood B is structured this way:

20 houses at	$210,000
20 houses at	$220,000
20 houses at	$230,000
20 houses at	$240,000
20 houses at	$250,000
20 houses at	$260,000
20 houses at	$280,000
20 houses at	$300,000
10 houses at	$350,000
10 houses at	$500,000

Neighborhood B is made up of 180 houses and also has a median home price of $250,000. However, the mean price for Neighborhood B is $287,777.

Even though the median and the mean taken together tell us something about each neighborhood, they don't tell us the high and low values, and we still don't know how many houses are priced at any particular level.

To illustrate this point, let's say you had $230,000 to spend on a house. Which neighborhood would you choose, based on the median and the mean?

Neighborhood B looks too expensive, but in fact, it isn't; there are 60 houses in or near your price range. Neighborhood A theoretically offers houses within your price range, but in reality, there aren't any—the 100 houses lower than $250,000 are all at $120,000, far below your budget and probably your wants. So remember that means and medians are just guides; they don't necessarily tell the whole story.

Mode. The mode is the most frequently found number in a group. There can be more than one mode. For example, in the same residential neighborhood, there might be several modes, such as $180,000, $240,000, and $350,000. These figures indicate that the supply of houses valued at those three prices is higher than the supply at any other price. One positive attribute of the mode is that it reflects *real* values, unlike the mean and median, which may be theoretical ones.

Sometimes the three averages are close together, or even the same, and sometimes not, depending on whether the distribution of all possible values is even or not. (The well-known bell curve exemplifies an even, or *normal*, distribution.)

Dennis G. Haack, in his book *Statistical Literacy: A Guide to Interpretation*, presents guidelines for the use of the three averages. The choice depends on the distribution of the data. The mean is best when the data are evenly distributed and there is only one mode (for example, when housing prices run the gamut, but may cluster around a particular price, such as $350,000). The median is best when there is only one mode, but the data are skewed (when there are a few houses in the over $5 million price range, but almost everything else is $750,000 or lower, and there is no clustering around a particular price). If we are interested in categorizing the data and there is more than one mode, the mode is best because it shows where most of the values lie. For example, if we were doing a market study of people who use 3-D software, we would find strong clustering by industry, such as architecture, film, advertising, and so on.

Always check to see which kind of average is being presented. If the documentation doesn't say, you can't assume it's the mean. The producer may have chosen the average that best supports his or her agenda, and, though technically accurate, that average may mislead.

When evaluating whether the type of average accurately represents the data, try to determine the range of values in the study. Are there any houses priced at $100,000? $2 million? Knowing the range will give you a better idea of the character of the area. Two completely different areas might exhibit the same median, for example, but one might range from $80,000 to $350,000, and another from $150,000 to $3 million. The former community is less affluent than the latter, or else the standard of living in the area is computed on a different scale.

Standard deviation. In order to understand the characteristics of data, statisticians employ ways of measuring the spread of numbers in a set of data. The measure of spread is called the standard deviation; its value indicates how the data are distributed. There are several different ways in which standard deviation can be assessed. Professional statisticians may employ more than one during an analysis. In general, the more closely grouped the data, the smaller the value of the standard deviation.

Percentiles. Percentiles indicate how data are distributed. A percentile is a number below which a certain percent of the data fall. For example, the 80th percentile is a number below which 80 percent of the values occur. If a selling price of $350,000 is the 80th percentile, then 80 percent of the houses in the area sell for less than $350,000. However, if a selling price of $750,000 is the 80th percentile, you're going to have to make a lot more money to afford to live in the neighborhood. Note that, in either case, the median value could be the same, though in reality that's unlikely.

Percentiles are useful in detecting possible abnormal conditions. For example, anything that lies below the fifth or above the 95th percentile has only a 1 in 10 chance of having occurred at random and should be looked at seriously.

Rates. A rate is a measure of the change of one thing over time. For example, the rate of inflation expresses the difference between a price index at an earlier time and a later time.

Ratings. A rating is a subjective measure of something that has been assigned a numerical value. For example, consider the familiar strain "On a scale of one to ten, where would you rate a CEO's performance?" Scales such as "agree strongly," "agree," "agree somewhat," "disagree somewhat," "disagree," "strongly disagree" are examples of ratings.

Nominal Data. Nominal data are expressed in categories that bear no ordered relationship to each other. An example of nominal data is race, as in Caucasian, African American, Native American, Hispanic, Pacific Islander, Asian, mixed race, etc. These categories cannot be grouped in any logical order other than alphabetically, though of course the values they contain can be.

Ordinal Data. Ordinal data are expressed in terms of categories that are related to each other, as in the previous CEO performance example, where categories are arranged by degree of agreement.

Probabilities. Probability is the likelihood that something will occur. Probability is calculated based on the number of times an event occurs when a random experiment is run many times.

Ratios. A ratio is one number divided by another. Ratios only make sense if the relationship between the numbers means something. For example, if one company's sales are $10 million and its competitor's sales are $20 million, the ratio of the first company's sales to those of the second company is 1:2. It makes no sense to draw a ratio between rankings of companies deemed the best to work for. The ratio 1:15 or vice versa, where number 1 is the highest ranked company and number 15 the 15th highest, doesn't provide meaningful information. One cannot say that company 1 is 15 times better to work for than company 15. Sometimes ratios are given without presentation of the raw numbers behind them. In that case, interpreting ratios requires the same caution as interpreting percentages: The situation can be overstated if small actual numbers are involved.

Interval Data. Like ordinal data, interval data are expressed in terms of categories that are related to each other. Unlike ordinal data, however, interval data exhibit meaningful differences from one category to the next. Interval data are used when there is no well-defined zero point, while ratio data, a subset of interval data, are used when such a point exists. You can say that one category of ratio is twice or half or some other numeric value more or less than another; with interval data, you cannot make the same claim. One example of interval data is time; types of ratio data include age and weight.

Methodologies for Gathering and Calculating Statistics

How do people count things? How can they say how many people watch broadcast TV? They never asked *me*! And how do they know how many miles people walk per week, or how much food is wasted by consumers? Common methodologies used for counting things follow.

Census

A census is a complete count of the thing or population to be measured. In theory, a census counts every single thing. However, in practice, a census can miss items. In the U.S. Census of Population and Housing, some people slip through the cracks. It is particularly difficult to count the homeless population, for example.

Surveys and Questionnaires

Samples

A sample is a representative "taste" of a group. A sample is a valid way of conducting a survey as long as it represents the group *without bias*, but not if it skews the characteristics found in the group. Samples may be used when a census is too expensive or impossible to implement.

A well-known, oft-questioned sample is that of the Kinsey report on human sexuality. Some people argue that anyone who would respond to such a survey will probably be less inhibited and more likely to experiment than the population at large.

Random Samples

Random samples are selected by chance. According to Darrell Huff in *How to Lie with Statistics*, the true test of whether a sample is random or not is whether any person or item in the group has an equal chance to be chosen. But, he explains, true random samples are so difficult and expensive to obtain that often variations on the random sample are used.

The larger the sample, the more precise the results. However, as the sample gets larger, the increase in rate of precision slows down. There comes a point at which increasing the size becomes more expensive but only minimally more effective. The *precision* of a sample is proportional to the square root of the sample size. See Table 2.1.

Table 2.1

Sample Sizes and Precision Rates		
Sample size (number of people)	Precision rate	Increase over the previous value of precision
100	10	N/A
200	14.14	41.4%
400	20	39.3%
600	24.49	22.5%
800	28.28	15.5%
1000	31.62	11.8%

Note that the largest increases in precision occur when the size of the sample is small. As you increase sample size, precision grows at a slower rate. Somewhere there is a point of diminishing returns; the trick is to find it and size the sample accordingly.

Panels

A panel is an ongoing survey. Panels are advantageous to the researcher because they provide more data than a one-shot survey, and they allow follow-up. For example, if panelists say they intend to do something, such as vote for a particular candidate or purchase a certain brand, the researcher can follow up to see if they really performed the action. Did those who said they were going to buy a new car within six months really do so?

What's wrong with this blurb?

Almost half of the U.K. population goes online on a daily basis.

According to a new study, 63 percent of U.K. Internet users who use the Net from either work or home go online to look for information.

Answer: The headline doesn't accurately portray the phenomenon being reported. It says that half the entire U.K. population goes online each day. The detail says that more than half of those who do go online do so to look for information, implying that the rest go online for some other purpose. In addition the 63 percent referred to in the detail doesn't match the "almost half" in the headline. Moreover, the detail doesn't mention the frequency with which the users go online, while the headline does.

If you read only the headline, you would draw a false conclusion.

Panels are good methods for measuring changes and time-dependent phenomena. For example, you can measure the change in attitude regarding a particular trend from one year to another *on an individual basis*. If a person likes the idea of solar energy tax credits at the time the law mandating them goes into effect, does he still approve a year later? The measurement is not how many people approved then and approve now, but of those who initially approved, how many still do and do not and what is the net change.

Panels may introduce distortion through the "re-interview" process. If a person has been asked about a topic before, he may become self-conscious when interviewed again. Sometimes panels and one-shot surveys are conducted in tandem to see if any re-interviewing distortion is occurring.

One pitfall of panels is dropouts due to death, personal resistance, moving, or other unavailability. This phenomenon may or may not affect the reliability of the study, depending on the magnitude of the loss and its effect on the thing being measured.

Observation

Observation involves looking at something. The observation itself may distort the data, as in a survey where people are ashamed or afraid to admit to membership in certain categories.

Experiment

An experiment is the process of observation or study that results in the collection of data.

Tests

A test measures the way something or someone performs compared to a standard. It may be a procedure designed to see if a piece of equipment works, or it may be a set of scorable questions. A test differs from a *questionnaire* in that the latter does not measure against a standard. Rather, a questionnaire produces a snapshot of attitudes, behavior, or experience.

Measurements

In the context of statistics, measurement means the use of instruments or devices to gather data.

Forecasting/Estimation

Forecasting is the use of known measurements to predict the value of unknown measurements that will occur in the future. An estimate is an approximation of an unknown value based on an extrapolation from a known value. Forecasting applies only to the future, while estimation may apply to past, current, or future measurements.

Derivation

Derivation involves extracting or reformatting information from the raw data. Index construction is one form of derivation. Changing units is another, as when you calculate a daily rate by dividing a yearly rate by 365.

Analysis

Analysis makes sense of the data and puts them in some context. One method of analysis is *correlation*, in which the relationship between two measurements is probed to see if they are causally related. For example, people who lose their hair are correlated with people who are tall, but that does not mean that height causes hair loss or that hair loss causes people to grow tall. The reason for the correlation is that height is correlated with sex, and men, who most often experience hair loss, tend to be taller than women.

Reading and Evaluating Data

Here are some factors to consider when looking at data with a critical eye.

The "Normal" Range for the Thing Being Counted

Are you counting something that normally occurs in high numbers? Low numbers? A large price increase for Toyota Camrys is much more significant than one for classic cars from the fifties. On the other hand, the launch of three people to Mars would be a much more significant event than hundreds of space shuttle flights.

The Starting Point

When dealing with increases and decreases, consider the location of the starting point. For example, if the price of a taco increases 43 percent from 35 cents to 50 cents, that sounds like a lot. However, the 35 cent price might have been a special offer or loss leader, and the jump may represent only a return to the regular price, which is the real starting point.

Retailers often advertise prices at 50 percent off. That sounds like a great deal, and it may be, but consider that markups on retail goods are enormous, so 50 percent off still could represent an adequate or substantial profit for the retailer.

Possible Rates of Change

To appreciate the significance of a number or percent, consider what's possible and/or likely for the thing being counted. For example, startup companies often log phenomenal rates of growth. However, mature companies do not, and probably cannot, rival those rates. If I say that a startup grew 400 percent in its first two years, and a mature company grew 5 percent, that doesn't necessarily mean that the mature company is doing poorly. Nor does it mean that the startup company is making a lot of money.

Factors Behind the Numbers

The numbers alone may not tell the story. For example, there might be spikes and precipitous drops due to uncommon events. A company's dramatic increase in market share may be astonishing and seemingly imply that the company is way out in front of its competitors. However, if that market share comes at the expense of revenue and/or profit, the numbers aren't nearly as impressive.

Self-Reports

Any time people report facts or opinions about themselves or others, there may be distortion. Sometimes distortion occurs because the respondent doesn't understand the question. Sometimes the person exaggerates for effect or to avoid embarrassment or to give a "positive" answer, and sometimes the person's memory is poor. And sometimes the interviewer can skew the results by affecting the subject's comfort level.

The accuracy of self-reports also depends to some extent on how the *questions* are phrased. Requests for exact information are less likely to be accurate than requests for ranges of information. For example, if you are asked how many hours per month you log on the Web, you might take a stab that may or may not be accurate. But if you're given ranges, such as 0–10, 11–20, 21–30, and more than 30 hours, your answers are more likely to represent your actual practice.

Misunderstood or hazy definitions can also skew results. What do "often," "sometimes," and "seldom" mean? Do they mean the same things to everyone? I can guarantee you that ASAP means an hour to some people and a week to others, and the meaning may vary with the situation.

Phrasing the Questions

Assumptions

The assumptions behind the questions must be valid for the results to be valid. Watch out for the old "When did you stop beating your wife?" type of question. It's one thing to ask, "If you have a favorite color, what is it?" and another to ask, "Do you prefer pink or green?" The former acknowledges the possibility that you may not have a favorite color and lets you specify any color you want, while the latter circumscribes your choices and changes the definition and scope of the thing being measured. If you hate both colors, is expressing a preference valid?

Look at the question and/or categories carefully, and if there seem to be skewed assumptions behind them, be suspicious, especially if there is no "none of the above" or "not applicable" alternative.

Leading Questions

The phrasing of questions may lead the respondent in a particular direction by pressuring a person to answer a certain way or to fail to consider other alternatives. Consider the following choices:

- Do you favor a socialist-type, government-run healthcare program?

- Do you favor a universal healthcare program administered by the government?

In the U.S, the use of the word "socialist" is extremely loaded and likely to produce a "No" response, whereas the concept of universal coverage implies equality and justice, concepts with which more people will agree.

Don't Know

The answer "Don't know" should not represent a large proportion of the answers. If it does, the questions weren't worded properly.

Self-reports by self-selected respondents are particularly suspicious. Those who volunteer for a study are unlikely to represent the characteristics of the general population. Volunteer respondents may have a particular agenda to advance or may be more outgoing and/or assertive than the average person. When you see that a study was composed of volunteers, be skeptical.

Definitions of Categories

Categories should not overlap. Ranges such as 0–5 and 5–10 are invalid, since the number 5 is included in both.

Significance

Significance is a measure of whether a statistical result could be due solely to random variation or whether there is an underlying relationship that will be seen in future trials.

Probable Error, Standard Error

Probable error and standard error tell you how accurate the data are.

Pitfalls
Specious or Biased Sources

Both researchers and respondents are sources, but in different ways. Either source may be biased or unreliable. When evaluating the statement, "Four out of five doctors recommend …," you must consider both producer and respondent. Which doctors are being cited? Doctors on the payroll of the company advertising the product? Doctors of philosophy? Doctors who belong to the American Medical Association? Who chose these doctors for the survey? According to what methodology were the doctors chosen?

Authority

Consider whether the source is authoritative for the thing being measured. Just because doctors supposedly chew a certain kind of gum doesn't necessarily make that gum better than others. And just because a reliable source produces the data doesn't mean that the conclusions drawn by the presenter are necessarily accurate.

Bias

Consider the possible bias of the producer. Can you trust a study of the safety of a product conducted by its manufacturer, or is an independent testing agency likely to be more reliable? Are figures put forth by a lobbying organization likely to be unbiased or presented in a neutral way?

In addition to ideological or personal-interest-based bias, there is also "unconscious bias," which may stem from personal or cultural assumptions. Until recently, most medical studies concentrated on men and had little or no female participation. It's not that the researchers were trying to snub women—they were simply unaware that many health conditions are gender-related.

Flabby Use of Words, Trick Words

Be wary of undefined terms, half-truths, and unfinished comparisons. Advertisers and producers who are honest and have nothing to hide will define their terms and give *complete* information.

Undefined Terms

Using the example of the doctors, what does "recommend" mean? Recommend such-and-such medicine compared to using no medicine at all? Or compared to similar medicines? And what constitutes a recommendation? A prescription? A statement within the confines of the examining room?

Half-Truths

Would you consider it fully truthful to refer to a single product as "recommended" when a doctor has listed a number of acceptable alternatives, such as "either Bufferin, Tylenol, or plain aspirin?"

Unfinished Comparisons

Beware of "more," "fewer," or "less" when not followed by "than ..." "More doctors recommend ..." means nothing without qualification. More doctors than cab drivers? More doctors recommend aspirin than chicken fat for headaches? Always ask "Than what?"

Emphasizing the Wrong Part of the Comparison

If I say that 5 percent of top management is dishonest, that sounds pretty awful. But if I say that 95 percent of top management is *not* dishonest, the situation sounds a lot more hopeful. Watch out for the following red flags.

Only, just, but: These words editorialize on the facts. If I say, "Only seven people in my high school class became doctors," I make it sound as though not very many people with whom I graduated became physicians. But when you consider that my class numbered 50 people, there's no "only" about it. If I wanted to be more accurate, I could have said, "Seven people in my high school class of 50 became doctors."

Fully: "Fully" is the opposite of "only," "just," and "but." Its use implies that a figure is unexpectedly high, as in, "Fully 86 percent of my high school class did *not* become doctors." This statement sounds intense, but 86 percent is actually on the low side when compared to the average. In most high schools, the percent of students who do not go on to become doctors is much higher than that. My use of "fully" misleads the reader into thinking there's something wrong with my class.

(Twice) as many: While technically accurate, this type of talk can be misleading. If I say "Twice as many of my friends bought new cars this year as last year," it sounds as though the auto manufacturers are cleaning up. However, last year *one* friend bought a car. This year, *two* people bought cars. Big deal!

(Twice) as likely: See "Twice as many."

Superlatives: "Most," "least," "fastest-growing," and the like may exaggerate the significance of the data.

Changing Definitions or Base Numbers (Comparing Apples to Something Other than Apples)

Definitions are critical. Counts don't mean a thing if the entity being counted conforms to one definition one time and another definition another time. For example, potential advertisers want to know how many people their ads will reach. If magazines report their paid circulation one time and the number of people who actually read the magazine another time, advertisers have no way of knowing exactly how many people they will reach.

The same precept holds true for base numbers. Inflation affects any number dealing with dollars, for example. When inflation is high, historical tables and charts presenting prices or expenditures make it appear as though spending and prices are high. The reverse is true for periods of low inflation. Therefore, statisticians use something called "constant dollars" to compensate for inflation.

This pitfall—comparing apples to oranges or something else—can affect presentation of statistics or can even infect the methodology itself. Watch out in both areas.

Flawed Analysis

Attributing causality where none exists. Here's one of my favorites. The assumptions are: "The higher the Gross Domestic Product (GDP), the healthier the economy" and "High GDPs mean prosperity." Not necessarily so, especially when you consider that subsumed under GDP are all kinds of negative exchanges of money, such as rising healthcare costs (and not necessarily a concomitant rise in the good health of the people), rebuilding costs from devastating natural disasters, rising costs of administering the criminal justice system and law enforcement due to rising crime, etc. People may be spending lots of money, but that doesn't necessarily mean they're enjoying a rising standard of living.

Assuming a rise in something itself when the real rise is in the reporting of the thing. Rape statistics might fall into this category. It is entirely possible that the incidence of rape itself has not increased, but that women are more willing to report rapes than they were in the past. However, the statistics alone might imply that the rape *rate* has increased more than it has.

False extrapolation. It is misleading to extrapolate survey results to a population that was not measured. A survey of attitudes about social issues in Massachusetts cannot be inferred to apply to Oklahomans as well.

It may also be dangerous to extrapolate based on historical statistics. Past performance is not *necessarily* an indication of future performance.

Throwing numbers out of proportion. Small differences between and among numbers may not be significant because of the degree of error contained in the survey. Don't let analysts exaggerate significance, and don't inflate importance based on your own perusal of the data.

Lack of Context

Misleading graphs and time series. Graphs that don't start at zero and graphs that aren't proportional are old tricks. Rises and falls can be exaggerated by extracting a range of numbers and making that range look like the whole picture. Dips and spikes also can be exaggerated if you count off measures in smaller units than normal. For example, a graph in which each square represents 10 is going to look far more dramatic than a graph in which each square represents 50.

The same caveat goes for time series that don't present information over a long enough span of time. While values may be accurate, the proper context is lacking.

Lack of information about the study and the conditions under which the study was performed. You won't be able to look for signs of flawed methodology if you don't have access to information about the study.

Flawed Methodology

Samples that are too small. Even if the producer doesn't misuse language, he or she may not have followed rigorous statistical methodology. A sample that is too small may yield just the results the surveyor wants to see, but those results may be invalid. Clue: high nonresponse rates are red flags.

Samples that are nonrepresentative. A sample must accurately represent the population being studied. It wouldn't be accurate to survey attitudes of women by talking only to those who live in big cities.

Contact methods that skew results. Telephone surveys may be suspect because they exclude people without access to phones, people who are rarely home, people who screen their calls, people with unlisted numbers, and so on. Door-to-door in-person surveys conducted on weekends are likely to exclude active people, or people who work on weekends, such as police officers, retail workers, and people in the performing arts.

Bad timing. Surveys should be taken at times when no influencing event has just occurred. For example, measuring investor sentiment right after the chairman of the Federal Reserve has expressed concern over the state of the economy is unlikely to yield a fair picture.

Gathering, presenting, and evaluating statistics accurately are essential if we are to avoid the "all statistics are lies" mentality. As a searcher for statistical information, you should note the red flags above and watch for pitfalls in the methodologies and presentation styles used by statistics gatherers. And you should be careful to evaluate the data and language used in describing statistics so that you do not fall into errors of misinterpretation.

For further information on evaluating data and its producers/publishers, be sure to see the superb book, *The Skeptical Business Searcher: The Information Advisor's Guide to Evaluating Web Data, Sites, and Sources*, by Robert Berkman, also from Information Today, Inc.

Chapter 3

Who Generates and Publishes Statistics?

The best searchers make educated guesses based on what they know about the landscape. Even if you aren't sure who produces the statistics you need, you'll be ahead if you can recognize a likely starting place. This chapter maps the landscape for you by introducing *types* of statistics generators and publishers. The subject-specific chapters that follow fill in by highlighting specific producers in particular fields.

The primary business statistics producers and publishers may be classified in the following broad and not mutually exclusive categories:

- Associations
- Companies
- Chambers of commerce and economic development organizations
- Economists, banks, and securities exchanges and brokerages
- Government agencies and international organizations
- Independent survey, polling, market research, and data organizations
- Publishers and media, including Web communities
- Nonprofit organizations
- Research centers

This chapter explains each of the categories and identifies sources for finding specific Web sites within them. Understanding who the producers are will give you a logical starting point in your quest.

Associations

Associations exist to look out for the interests of their members. Trade associations advance the business and financial interests of those working within a particular business or industry. Professional associations contribute to the body of knowledge necessary for practicing a particular profession, attempt to keep members' skills and expertise up-to-date, and try to promote a positive image of the profession. Sometimes the lines between trade and professional associations blur, as in the case of the American Hospital Association.

Statistics help associations monitor the environment within which they operate, identify trends, and conduct strategic planning. Many associations lobby, and statistics help persuade. Sometimes statistics are kept in-house; sometimes they appear in the association's journal, as a separate publication, or on the organization's Web site.

United States

American Society of Association Executives, http://www.asaenet.org/main. Select the gateway to associations.

Associations on the Net from the Internet Public Library, http://ipl.sils.umich.edu/ref/AON

Directory of Associations from Business Know-How, http://www.businessknowhow.com/associations/search_associations.asp

Directory of Associations from Concept Marketing Group, Inc., http://www.marketingsource.com/associations. Lists more than 34,000 associations around the world. Searching and basic information are free. Detailed information requires a subscription. $

Google, http://directory.google.com/Top/Business/Resources/Associations. Google lists associations under a variety of categories. The URL here leads to business-related associations.

The Virtual Community of Associations, http://www.vcanet.org/vca/assns.htm. Associations located in the greater Washington, DC area.

Yahoo! Trade Associations, http://dir.yahoo.com/Business_and_
Economy/Organizations/Trade_Associations. Multinational.

Australia and New Zealand

Business Organisations from PIPERS New Zealand Pages, http://
www.piperpat.co.nz/nz/business/organs.html

Government and Business Associations Directory, Australia,
http://www.business.gov.au

New Zealand Associations from BizInfo, http://www.bizinfo.co.nz

Yahoo! Australia and New Zealand, http://au.dir.yahoo.com/
business_and_economy/organisations/Trade_Associations

Canada

Associations Canada, http://circ.micromedia.ca

Canadian Associations from the Quebec Association of Export
Trading Houses, http://www.amceq.org/Tools/en_association.htm

Hillwatch Directory of Associations, Interest Groups, NGOs,
Coalitions, and Corporations, http://www.hillwatch.com/lobbylist/
LobbyHome.htm. Canadian and world information.

Yahoo! Canada, http://ca.dir.yahoo.com/business_and_economy/
organizations/Trade_Associations

Ireland

Yahoo! U.K. and Ireland, http://uk.dir.yahoo.com/business_and_
economy/organisations/trade_associations

United Kingdom and Northern Ireland

Directory of U.K. Trade Associations, http://www.brainstorm.co.uk/
TANC/Directory/Welcome.html

Trade Association Forum, http://www.taforum.org

Yahoo! U.K. and Ireland, http://uk.dir.yahoo.com/business_and_economy/organisations/trade_associations

Europe

Civil Society Organisations from the European Commission, http://europa.eu.int/comm/civil_society/coneccs/index_en.htm. European associations and interest groups.

Yahoo! European Organizations, http://dir.yahoo.com/Regional/Regions/Europe/Business_and_Economy/Organizations

Yahoo! Regions, http://dir.yahoo.com/Regional/Regions. See individual regions and countries, Business and Economy, then Organizations.

You can also conduct a Google search using keywords you think should be in the association's name plus words like "association," "society," and "federation."

Companies

Private and public companies conduct their own market research. Usually they hold this information close to the chest, but sometimes they make it public in their annual reports, on their Web sites, and at conferences and trade shows. Sometimes private research comes out during litigation, and if so, there may be media coverage of it. You can also find company-produced market information in trade magazine articles, newspapers, and speech and interview transcripts.

Of course, companies also produce financial and other information about themselves, their operations, and their goals. Public companies are required to file their financials with government regulatory bodies such as the Securities and Exchange Commission in the U.S. and Companies House in the United Kingdom. In some countries, private companies are required to do so as well. However, in those countries that don't force private companies to file their information, figures can be hard to get. In those cases, you will need to consult news articles and press releases and also do some detective work. For more information on estimating private company financials, see Chapter 12.

Chambers of Commerce and Economic Development Organizations

Chambers of commerce may be international, national, or local. They produce demographics and economic information, which may or may not be found online.

Other economic development organizations may use words like *advancement*, *development*, *small business*, *commerce*, *leadership*, and *industry* in their names.

Economists, Banks, and Securities Exchanges and Brokerages

Following the economy is critical to banks, brokerage houses, and other financial institutions. Researchers, usually professional economists, follow trends and often derive useful statistics from them.

Government Agencies

Government agencies are perhaps the best-known and most prolific sources of statistics. Because information is so vital to policy planning and decision-making, not to mention daily operations, government agencies collect, tally, and analyze data on everything from demographics to traffic flow. The main caveat regarding government statistics is that they tend not to be very specific. If you want very detailed information, you will need to go to associations, trade journals, and market research reports.

Every level of government generates statistics. Most now have Web sites, at least in the English-speaking countries emphasized in this book. Governments may collect statistics through special surveys and censuses, or they may do so as a byproduct of other activities. For example, trade data are generated when customs forms are filled out. The decennial U.S. census was originally created to serve a constitutional function: to apportion the membership of the House of

Representatives according to populations and distributions of people throughout the states. Now census data is used for just about every government function, and lots of business, health, environmental, and other applications, too.

National Government

At the national level, statistics are generated by cabinet- or ministry-level agencies, independent agencies, and/or national statistical agencies. Often there are agencies within agencies, or bureaus within agencies, or other subdivisions, which can be confusing if you do not understand government organization. Some organizations use each other's data to produce their own byproducts or analyses. By sharing resources, they are able to save money.

National governments have agencies that cover functions such as the following:

Agriculture
- Commodity prices
- Demand
- Economic and environmental indicators relating to agricultural production and resource use
- Farm acreage
- Farm wages and employment
- Food aid
- Foreign market research
- Growing conditions
- Indicators of food and consumer issues
- Movement volume
- Production, supply, and prices of crops and livestock
- Quality
- Socioeconomic indicators of the farm sector and rural economies
- Supply, demand, and performance of domestic and international agricultural and food markets
- Trade data

Commerce

- Balance of payments
- Corporate profits
- Direct investment abroad
- Foreign investment in the U.S.
- GDP
- Global trade outlook
- Goods and services trade
- National and regional income and wealth
- National and state personal income
- Products by industry
- Sales and inventories
- State exports
- Statistics for various industry groups, including employment, wages, capital expenditures, and trade
- Trade
- Trade for various countries

Census

- Agriculture
- Healthcare
- Housing
- Industry
- Manufacturing
- Migration/immigration
- Population and vital statistics
- Tax revenues
- Trade
- Transportation
- Wealth and poverty

- Energy
- Demand and consumption
- Energy distribution
- Energy resource reserves
- Energy trends and economic effects of those trends on regional and industrial sectors
- Production
- Technology

Health and Welfare

- Healthcare benefits
- Healthcare expenditures
- Healthcare utilization
- Prices
- Employment
- Immunizations
- Diagnostics
- Managed care
- Incidences of diseases
- Pharmaceuticals and devices
- Vital statistics

Labor

- Compensation
- Consumer expenditures
- Employment
- Occupational safety and health
- Prices
- Productivity
- Working conditions

Patents and Trademarks
- Intellectual property

Transportation
- Aviation
- Highways
- Maritime transportation
- Mass transit
- Railroads

Treasury
- Customs
- Public debt
- Taxes

Other
- Banking
- Communications
- Consumer issues
- Environmental protection
- Government accounting and budget
- Intelligence and law enforcement
- Nuclear issues
- Postal service
- Science
- Securities
- Small business
- Social security
- Space
- Trade

A number of metasites have been created to facilitate access to government Web sites and official statistics agencies. Some useful metasites follow.

United States

FedStats, http://www.fedstats.gov. A gateway to statistics offered by U.S. government agencies.

FirstGov, http://www.firstgov.gov. Gateway to the U.S. Federal government.

U.S. State Data Centers, http://www.census.gov/sdc/www

Australia

Australian Bureau of Statistics, http://www.abs.gov.au/Ausstats/abs @.nsf/ausstatshome

Australian Commonwealth Government Information, http://www. fed.gov.au/KSP. Includes links to both commonwealth and state/ territory Web sites.

Canada

Government of Canada, http://canada.gc.ca. Includes links to both national and provincial/territory governments.

Statistics Canada, http://www.statcan.ca

Ireland

Central Statistics Office Ireland, http://www.cso.ie

Government of Ireland, http://www.irlgov.ie. Includes links to both state agencies and local authorities.

New Zealand

New Zealand Government Online, http://www.govt.nz. Includes links to both Government of New Zealand and local government sites.

Statistics New Zealand, http://www.stats.govt.nz

United Kingdom and Northern Ireland

The Government of Northern Ireland, http://www.nics.gov.uk

Northern Ireland Statistics and Research Agency (NISRA), http://www.nisra.gov.uk. Official Northern Ireland statistics.

U.K. Government Online, http://www.ukonline.gov.uk. Includes links to both federal and local agencies.

U.K. National Statistics Office, http://www.statistics.gov.uk

Europe

European Governments Online, http://europa.eu.int/abc/governments/index_en.html

The European Union, http://europa.eu.int

State and Local Governments

State and local data centers often team up with federal agencies or each other to distribute information relating to the region in question.

State-level agencies that generate statistics often parallel federal government functions, with some exceptions, such as defense. Areas that normally deal with state level include:

Business and Financial
- Banking
- Commerce
- Corporations
- Economic development

- Employment
- Insurance
- Licensing of professionals
- Real estate
- Taxes

Physical Services
- Agriculture
- Conservation
- Emergency services
- Environment (pollution, water and air quality, hazardous materials, forestry, fish and game, deserts, etc.)
- Housing
- Parks and recreation
- Public utilities
- Transportation and highways

Social Services
- Consumer affairs
- Education
- Health and mental health
- Substance abuse
- Veterans
- Welfare

In some cases special agencies also exist, such as those dealing with women's issues, aging, lotteries, mining, horse racing, fairs, sports, alcoholic beverages, political practices, arts and culture, and boating and waterways. States also deal with matters such as hunting and fishing and guns.

Local Governments
City, town, county, and parish functions include physical services such as:

- Airports
- Fire control
- Harbors
- Hospitals and clinics
- Sanitation
- Traffic and roads
- Utilities

International Organizations

Many international organizations, such as the United Nations and the International Monetary Fund, are quasi-governmental and generate statistics in the same ways that governments do. While the United Nations and its agencies are major international statistics-makers, international chambers of commerce and associations also count things and track business conditions. (For a helpful set of links to international chambers of commerce, see http://www.worldchambers. com.) International alliances such as the European Union and the Organization of American States also produce statistics.

Independent Survey, Polling, Market Research, and Data Organizations
Survey and Polling

Everyone has heard of Gallup polls and Nielsen ratings. Companies like Gallup and Nielsen are private survey organizations that conduct demographic and attitude research for a fee. Newspapers and broadcast media, such as the *Los Angeles Times* and CNN, often conduct polls, frequently on topics of interest to the public such as smoking, crime, race, and even standards of beauty. Examples of polling organizations include:

- The Gallup Organization, http://www.gallup.com
- Louis Harris and Associates, http://www.harrisinteractive.com
- The Pew Research Center for the People and the Press, http://www. people-press.org

- Roper Center for Public Opinion Research, http://www.lib.uconn.edu/RoperCenter
- The Washington Post, http://www.washingtonpost.com

Market Research

Market research organizations play a critical role in supporting business by providing information on actual and potential demand for products and services.

Market research may include major industry studies, customer satisfaction surveys, "would you buy this?" research, demographics, technological trends, and studies of the economy and business environments in general. You will find some market research organizations with worthwhile Web sites listed in Chapter 7.

Publishers and Media, Including Web Communities

One of your best bets for business statistics is trade journals. These publications track industry developments so their readers can make informed decisions. You will find many listings for trade journals in the chapters that follow: publications like *Variety*, which covers the entertainment industry; *Advertising Age* for advertising; *Drug Topics*, *Progressive Grocer*, and *Wireless Week*. In addition, national and regional newspapers and magazines can be very helpful, especially the *Wall Street Journal*, *Business Week*, the *Los Angeles Business Journal*, and their ilk.

You will also want to check out online-only media, such as *Digital Media Net* (http://www.digitalmedianet.com) and Plastics.com (http://www.plastics.com).

To identify trade journals, check the lists of journals covered by aggregators, such as:

Dialog, http://www.dialog.com. Go into the database catalog (select Sources, then Dialog and Dialog DataStar, then Dialog Database Catalog). You want the section on Search Aids and Source Lists, which starts on page 310 of the 2002 catalog. The list of 7,000 sources is voluminous, comprehensive, and alphabetically arranged, but you can search the PDF file by keywords and/or glance through it quickly. You don't have to be a subscriber to view this information.

Factiva, http://www.factiva.com. Select Products, then Dow Jones Interactive, then Article Archive. Then click on "Search the Publications Library source list."

FindArticles, http://www.FindArticles.com. Drill down by subject.

ProQuest, http://www.proquest.com. Under Products, select Business. You can choose from a variety of databases. Click on "More Product Information," then look for the title lists.

Or, you can consult directories like:

Google, http://www.google.com. Click on the Directory tab, then Business, News and Publications, Magazines. From there you can select Trade or look at the individual listings, which cover a variety of countries. Or start with Regional at the top level and follow the same strategy to get to countries and regions around the world.

Yahoo!, http://www.yahoo.com. Go to Business and Economy, then News and Media. Select Magazines, then Trade Magazines, then the category in which you are interested. Consult the Yahoo! sites for various countries as well by selecting Regional from the top level menu, then following the same strategy.

Interest Groups and Nonprofit Organizations
Interest Groups

Interest groups exist to promulgate a particular point of view through the political process, and, to support their arguments, they conduct surveys and compile statistics. You'll find everyone from the Sierra Club to the National Rifle Association measuring things. Advocacy organizations such as Americans for a Balanced Budget and the League of Conservation Voters are not the only groups that lobby or recommend political action. Many associations pursue political action as well, such as the American Medical Association and the American Library Association.

For lists of advocacy groups in the U.S., consult PoliticsOL.com at http://www. politicsol.com, Political Advocacy Groups at http://www.csuchico.edu/~kcfount, and the Society/Activism category in the Google directory at http://directory.google. com. Of course, you can also search the Web using Google.

For advocacy groups in various countries, see Idealist.org at http://www. idealist.com or http://www.idealist.org, or search the Web using Google. You can also drill down into country information using the Google directory.

Nonprofit Organizations

People come together for all kinds of reasons, not just for politics and religion. You'll find everything from comic book clubs to the Japan Center for Intercultural Communications generating statistics for the use of their members and the public.

Universities

University-related producers include professors who conduct research and publish reports, papers, and books; graduate students; libraries and librarians; and special organizations, such as the Office of Population Research at Princeton University. Sometimes universities team up with other entities, such as governments, hospitals, and private companies, to compile and publish statistics.

Research Centers

Research centers, like universities, are rich sources of statistics in many of the same ways. While most are connected with universities and government agencies, some are independent.

To identify research centers, consult Google at http://www.google.com. Go to the top level of the Google Directory by clicking on the Directory tab, then search or drill down by subject.

With so many different entities generating statistics, it's natural to think that just about every numerical fact must be available somewhere. Unfortunately, that isn't so, but to increase your chances of success, you should attempt to determine who might have collected that information. This chapter gives you a framework with which to determine possible sources to find statistics. The next chapter will give some tips on how to ferret them out once you've decided on a source.

Chapter 4

General Search Tips

In *Finding Statistics Online*, I offered all kinds of fancy tips for statistics searching on the Web. While many of those suggestions are still valid, I would like to replace a large portion of them with one very effective strategy: Use the Google search engine (http://www.google.com) to look for both extremely specific and general statistics.

And so I present you with **Tip Number One:** Use the Google search engine. Google wasn't available when I wrote *Finding Statistics Online*. In those days, using a Web search engine to look for a specific statistic was a prescription for failure. No longer. Chances are very good that Google will lead you to the right place in a hurry. Combine that with a fast Internet connection, and you'll be more productive than you dreamed possible.

Tip Number Two: Use phrase searching whenever possible. This technique more than any other helps you narrow down your search to the most relevant items. Many systems designate phrases with quotes, as in "business statistics." Be sure to check the rules to make sure that you are indeed telling the search engine to look for phrases.

Tip Number Three: Don't worry about subscriptions to Web sites, except in the case of Factiva. Unless you are a librarian or other information professional who searches all day long, you don't need one. Pay-per-view services make all the old folderol unnecessary. Factiva, one of the best, requires a $69 annual password fee, but the $2.95 per-article fee is hard to beat. Factiva is an excellent collection for you, covering news, business journals, press releases, and trade journals. Other worthwhile aggregators are FindArticles (http://www.FindArticles.com) and eLibrary (http://www.elibrary.com).

Tip Number Four: Consult trade journals and industry associations. You can start with the lists in Chapters 5 and 6—U.S. and Non-U.S. Industry Sources, respectively. If the lists don't help, use Google to search for journals and/or associations, using words you think might appear in the name. You can also identify associations by consulting Web site directories of trade shows. Once you have done so, if you can't find what you're looking for on their Web sites, call them. Okay, that isn't business statistics solely on the Web, but you want them, don't you? When you call a journal, ask for the library and/or editorial, then ask whether they have or know of statistics on your topic. Often they will be too busy to talk to you or will not be open to the public, but sometimes you will connect with a sympathetic person who will make your life easier. When you call associations, be sure you've spoken to the correct person before you give up. Do not take the word of the receptionist as the final answer.

Tip Number Five: Don't procrastinate when it comes to phone calls. If you can't find exactly what you need on a Web site, call to see if the organization has more information. Remember, however, that it can take days to get hold of a real person.

Tip Number Six: Always follow toeholds. If the Web site you've found does not have what you need, it may list resources that can help you.

Developing an Effective Strategy
Tips for Searching Full Text

Here is something else that has changed since *Finding Statistics Online* was published. You can now find needles in haystacks easily using Google, Factiva, and other search engines. I am so excited about the following technique that I can't wait to tell you about it!

Consider the sentence "There are one million lawyers in the United States." In *Finding Statistics Online*, I advised you to forget about finding sentences like that because there's so little that is distinctive about them. The words "there," "are," "in," and "the" are stop words, that is, words that search engines ignore. You could have searched on the remaining terms like "lawyers" and "United States" until you were blue in the face without answering the question "How many lawyers are there in the United States?" However, using phrase searching, you can now zero in on the answer quickly. All you need to do is look for phrases within the sentence "There are one million lawyers in the United States" or variations therein, including the stop words, which the search engine takes seriously as long as you make them part of a phrase:

On Google: *"there are" "lawyers in the United States"*

On Factiva: there are AND lawyers in the United States

Now you can successfully use phrases such as:

"percent of adults believe that"

"aerospace industry revenues"

"Microsoft earned" "last year"

"Pfizer's market share"

"million people have purchased"

I also urge you to try putting the current year in your search statement if the system provides no way for you to limit by date. While this strategy doesn't always work, it can help confine your results to the most recent articles. If you get too few hits this way, take the date out and search again.

Try it right now!

Here are some more keywords you may find useful:

- Statistics
- Market share
- Index(es)/indices

- Market research
- Numeric
- Financial data
- Sales
- Forecasts
- Demographics
- Market size
- Expenditures
- Costs
- Industry overview
- Prices
- Age(s)

Sometimes the word *trends* can be helpful, though it may indicate description rather than quantification.

Units/Measures

- Percent or per cent. Beware! Sometimes the percent sign (%) is used, and it is not searchable in most online systems.
- Rate/rated/rating(s)
- Hundred
- Thousand
- Million
- Billion
- The unit you're measuring, such as *copies* for books, *sales*, *dollars*, etc.
- Odds
- Chance(s)
- Probability

Trends

Use these words, in various tenses, to help isolate text with numeric content.

- Increase(d)
- Decrease(d)
- Grow/grew
- Decline(d)
- Rise(n)
- Fall(en)

Comparisons

- As much as
- As many, as in "twice as many"
- As likely, as in "twice as likely"
- More likely
- Less likely
- Largest
- Smallest
- Most
- Least
- Fastest-growing
- Top, as in "The Top 100 Companies"

Other

- Found/finds/reports that, as in "A study has found that ..."
- According to, as in "According to a study ..."
- Is estimated at
- Says, as in "A study released by XYZ says ..."

Using Web Sites Effectively

Many Web sites are arranged by people with, shall we say, less than a complete understanding of your needs. However, there are certain flags you can look for that will often signal the presence of useful information. Here are some of the terms or links you'll want to try:

- Annual report(s)
- Archive
- Bulletin(s)
- Data (The word *data* is sometimes used interchangeably with *statistics*. You may see the term *data collection(s)* or *data series*.)
- Databases
- Facts, factsheets
- FAQ (frequently asked questions)
- Industry overview
- Library
- News
- Papers
- Poll
- Press releases
- Publications
- Reports
- Research
- Series
- Statistics
- Study
- Summaries
- Survey
- Time series
- Trend(s)

Look for names of particular reports, such as "State of the ..." Often these documents cover particular time periods, so make sure the date on the report is recent. Sometimes you will have to use the search engine at the site, browse lists of publications or indices, or look through the online journal/paper collection.

If the text on your screen is particularly dense, use your browser's Find feature to search for keywords.

Specific Sources or Sections

Focusing in on particular sources, or relevant sections of particular sources, is a good way to eliminate extraneous material. You may want to identify a journal and confine the search just to it, or limit your search to the financial or business section of a newspaper.

Tips for Searching Factiva, FindArticles, and eLibrary

Factiva

To use Factiva, you'll need a basic understanding of its syntax. My best advice to you is to use phrase searching and proximity. You will rarely need anything else, except perhaps truncation.

Phrase searching. This technique is easier than easy on Factiva. Phrases are simply words strung together with spaces between them, as in *business statistics*. Voila! In addition, Factiva's new *Standard* search screen includes the ability to utilize Factiva's proprietary taxonomy, Factiva Intelligent Indexing, to build the targeted searches based on Company, Industry, Region, and Subject codes.

Proximity. My favorite technique is to use the "W/n" operator. This expression means that words must appear within n words of each other, in that exact order. You should have a basic understanding of article and English language sentence structure to use this operator. If you don't think you understand where various types of information appear in journalistic reports, look through your newspaper or news magazine to get a good feel for how things are phrased and structured. The title should be, but isn't always, descriptive of the main point.

The lead paragraph elaborates on the main point—usually. The rest of the article includes details and tangents.

Here's how to use proximity. If I say *business w/2 statistics*, the word "business" must appear either next to, one word in front of, or two words in front of the word "statistics." You can specify any number for n, but I think any amount over 10 is too much. You can also use Factiva's other proximity operators, though I rarely do. These include NEARn, which means that the words or phrases must appear within n number of words of each other in any order, and SAME, which means that the words or phrases must appear in the same paragraph. Frankly, the latter holds little utility for me. If words appear within the same paragraph, they should probably be pretty close to each other or else it doesn't matter that much whether they are in the same paragraph or the same document.

Truncation. Sometimes you will find it useful to stub off a word that can appear in different forms rather than having to specify each variation. This feat is accomplished by using the $ operator. For example, if I say *comput$*, I will pick up all terms that start with "comput," including "computer," "computers," and "computing." I personally use truncation primarily for specifying the singular and plural form of a word in one go. I could also say *computer or computers*. It really doesn't matter which way you do it.

As for the other options, you can look them up on the Factiva search page, but I doubt you will need them. It is far more important to understand which dates, publications, and part of a document you are searching.

Date searching. Factiva allows you to select "Current Year," Current Month," "All Dates," or a range of dates that you specify. Be careful that your date selection is set the way you want it. The system defaults to "Current Year." When looking for statistics, you may have to go back a bit in time. You can start current, but don't give up if you don't find anything. Many statistics aren't published regularly, so you may have to try further back in time. Be aware, however, that if you go too far back, the statistics may be too old to be useful.

Publications. Factiva provides several options. The default is "All Content," which is the broadest search possible and includes material from a variety of industries and countries. However, you can also create custom publication lists. Select Major News and Business Publications for statistics likely to be reported nationally or worldwide. Factiva also groups publications by type (Dow Jones publications, media transcripts, top 50 U.S. newspapers, etc.), major industry, and world region. You can select one or more groups at a time. You can also opt for all languages (there are 22 of them), or specify one or several languages.

To select only one publication, simply click on one of the previous options and then the publication you want, and you'll get a search screen that covers just that item. For example, if I click on "Media & Entertainment," I can isolate the *Hollywood Reporter.* A particularly useful feature for those who select one publication at a time is the ability to browse recent headlines and their lead sentences for free. You are more restricted in single-publication searches, however. You cannot specify dates or portions of the article to search, though you can use all the standard operators like "W/n."

Searching parts of a document. Factiva allows you to search article headlines, lead paragraphs, headline and lead paragraph, or the full article. Frankly, I use "headline and lead paragraph" and "full article" almost exclusively. The former allows you to get a good sense of the main topic of the article. The latter lets you fish for snippets. There is little reason to search headlines alone because they are usually too short to be useful. I can't see why anyone would search the lead paragraph by itself.

Let me remind you that not all articles are available immediately after publication. Though some are, particularly those from daily newspapers, others can take weeks or a month or two to show up. For specifics, check the source page for the individual publication in question if you know which one you want. This time lag may explain your inability to find something you know has been published very recently. If you are absolutely sure you saw something and you know where it was, check the Web site for that particular publication outside Factiva.

FindArticles

There are a couple of tricks to searching FindArticles.

First, since the system doesn't allow you to specify a date range, you should put the current and perhaps the previous year in with your search terms. This strategy won't narrow your search to those years exclusively, but it might help cut out some of the junk.

Second, be aware that while you can specify a group of magazines or all magazines, if you do the former, the system knocks you back to the "all" option on your results screen. If you want to keep searching your group, you will have to reset the drop-down menu. You can search one particular publication by looking at a specific article from that publication, then selecting "Search this Magazine" next to the publication name. An adjacent link leads you directly to the publication's Web site.

Phrase searching is accomplished by putting your phrase in quotes, as in *"business statistics."* To make sure that your terms must appear in the article (equivalent to the AND Boolean operator), you must put a plus sign in front of each of them, as in *+airline +revenues.* You can also say *+ "airline revenues"* if you prefer to use the phrase rather than two separate terms. Of course, doing so makes your search more focused.

Using terms without quotes or plus signs means that only one of them must appear in each article. So if I say *airline revenues*, I might find articles only about airlines or only about revenues, but not necessarily about airline revenues.

Like Factiva, FindArticles is also slightly hampered by a time lag, so if you want something from today or last week, you may have to go directly to the site of the publication in question.

eLibrary

eLibrary is a cinch to use, but you may need to supplement it with other systems. Its thousands of sources comprise an impressive collection, but it suffers from holes in coverage. For example, while offering standard newspapers and journals like *Computerworld*, *New England Economic Review*, and *Christian Science Monitor*, eLibrary does not afford access to *Wall Street Journal*, *Los Angles Times*, and *Aviation Week*. It does, however, offer radio and television transcripts of shows such as *60 Minutes* and *Weekly Edition* (NPR) plus the full text of reference books such as almanacs and a series on facts about working women.

eLibrary accommodates natural language searching (*What is Tropicana's market share?*), phrase searching (put the phrase inside double quotes, e.g., *"aviation industry revenues"*), and Boolean (AND, OR, AND NOT, e.g., *3D AND revenues*). Before you begin, you must select the media type(s): newspapers, magazines, transcripts, pictures (yes, pictures!), books, and/or maps. You can limit by date, publication, or author: select Refine Search.

Pricing at press time was $14.95 per month or $79.95 per year, and that includes everything. A real bargain.

Systems for Librarians and Information Professionals

For tips on searching systems for librarians and information professionals, see the author's book *Finding Statistics Online*.

Extended Case Study:
The Size of the Computer Games Industry

Purpose: This case study demonstrates how to use a search engine, an association, an article aggregator, and an industry Web site to determine the size of an industry.

Sources Used: Google, Interactive Digital Software Association, Factiva, Gamasutra

I decided to start with Google because it is powerful and far-reaching. I used the following terms: *computer games industry billion*, choosing them because I knew the industry size is in the billions of dollars. One alternative, *computer games industry size*, would have been reasonable, but it seemed less direct, and in fact, I got nothing useful on the first page using it. (If you don't find something on the first page with Google, your chances of doing so fall precipitously—with that particular strategy.) I got a number of relevant-looking hits, but a quick glance at sources and dates eliminated some of them right away. For example, the first two sites were from names I didn't recognize. I thought that if I could find a big name I trusted, I'd be better off. The third site was also something I didn't recognize (http://www.game-research.com), but it sounded intriguing, so I took a look.

It turns out that Game Research is the site of a couple of consultants. Ordinarily, I'd be skeptical about accepting the validity of statistics on such a site, but here, the statistics on market size included a link to a source I do know: the Interactive Digital Software Association, or IDSA. The statistics cited came from year 2000 though, which was a while ago. Sometimes numbers that are a couple of years old are the best you can do, but computer games are hot, and I knew I could do better. I clicked through to see if the IDSA had anything more recent.

The link took me to a PDF file containing a state-of-the-industry report for 2000 to 2001. I know that there are more recent statistics on the games industry—I've read them in the *Wall Street Journal* and other places. I decided to see whether the IDSA has more recent statistics elsewhere. To get to the association's home page, I edited the site's URL down from http://www.idsa.com/releases/SOTI2001.pdf to http://www.idsa.com and clicked.

The home page had these links: Media center, IDSA programs, Members, Anti-piracy, and Government Affairs. I'm sure you can see right away that the only link with any potential here is "Media center" because it could lead us to press releases and facts about the industry. Voilá! That's exactly what we got—both of them. A link to "Top Ten Industry Facts" and a press release entitled "Essential facts about the video and computer game industry" led to the same answer: In 2001, the size of the video and computer games industry worldwide was $6.35 billion.

I was skeptical. I know this industry, and I could have sworn that somewhere I saw a figure exceeding $9 billion. I thought I'd better verify IDSA's findings. Since I read the *Wall Street Journal* every day, it was likely I'd seen the higher figure there. I would go to Factiva to see what the *Journal* had to say on the subject.

I didn't worry about confining my search to the *Journal* alone, but I did check the box that says "Major News & Business Publications" to keep the search from going too broad. The games industry is major news these days, so the national media should cover it well.

In the search box, I typed the following: *computer w/1 games w/1 industry w/10 billion*. I set the year to "current," and specified "full text." I got only one article, which was a bit disconcerting. There should have been more. It was:

Value of playing computer games

The New Straits Times, 05/09/2002, 950 words.
If you ask game publishers about the value of playing computer games, they are likely to give it a two thumbs-up. And why not? For them, computer games are part of an industry that churns over US$1...

The date was recent. And those ellipses looked like they might be hiding the industry size. These were good signs. But the publication was from Australia. Was it possible that the figures were for that country only? No way to know without looking.

It turned out that the figures were indeed only for Australia, despite being expressed in U.S. dollars:

"Computer games are part of an industry that churns over US$1 billion (RM3.8 billion) in annual revenues."

Something didn't compute. I knew that the global industry is larger than $1 billion. Could this be the figure for Australia? I couldn't tell by reading the rest of the article. Further, technically I shouldn't have retrieved this article because the word "industry" was not within one word of the word "games." Or was it? Notice that the words between "games" and "industry" include only one word of substance: "part." The others, "are," "of," and "an," are stop words—they don't count. Tricky!

The search was too restrictive. I broadened it a little by taking out the word "industry." A strategy like *computer w/1 games w/10 billion* might get more hits. It did—12, to be exact.

I found:
Cash prizes

The Times of London, 04/11/2002, 168 words.
The games industry is worth more than Pounds 14 billion worldwide, say the analysts. In the U.K. alone last year, the computer-games market was worth Pounds 1.6 billion, according to the European ...

This article was fairly recent, and I could see instantly that I had a global figure: 14 billion pounds sterling. But this was a strange number. Since the pound was worth about $1.50 U.S., that made the global industry about $21 billion. How can that be? I was sure it was $9 billion. (Note the fact that the industry in the U.K. is worth 1.6 billion pounds implies that the figure of $1 billion in the Australian article describes the size of the Australian computer games market.) The source was the European Leisure Software Publishers Association

I decided it was time to home in on the *Journal*, since I was pretty sure I saw that $9 billion number there.

In order to limit my search to the *Journal*, I clicked on the name of the paper right below "Major News & Business Publications" to get a search page that confined my query to that source.

I made a very broad search just for openers to see what I get: *computer w/1 games.*

There were 68 hits. Three interested me:

Consoles Outrun Computers
The Wall Street Journal, 04/19/2002, 1065 words.
IF THE BATTLE for the living room being waged by Microsoft Corp., Nintendo Co. and Sony Corp. were an auto-racing videogame, the contest would be too early and too close to call. But as their videogame ...

This article was recent and long, and the fact that both consoles and PCs were named implied that there were figures for both. A good possibility.

Technology (A Special Report) --- Play Time: Online games are booming; And ...

The Wall Street Journal, 03/05/2002, 2024 words.
NORM VANCE plays computer games. But he doesn't slay digital dragons or nuke invading aliens, or even guide a skateboard through the virtual perils. ...

This article was recent enough, but treated online games. Did that mean it quantified the PC and console markets as well? There was no way to tell without retrieving the whole article.

Video-Game Industry Is Seen Expanding At a Rapid Clip During Next Five...
The Wall Street Journal, 05/25/2001, 458 words.
LOS ANGELES -- Sales for the global-entertainment games industry are expected to rise 71%, or $85.7 billion, during the next five years, according to a study...

This article was getting a bit old. Also, what was this $85 billion number? Was it possible the industry could grow that much in five years? How was the author defining "global-entertainment games industry?"
I decided to retrieve all three articles.

The First Article

Within the first article, I found:

"Buoyed in large part by low-price consoles, U.S. sales of videogames rose a staggering 43% to $9.4 billion in 2001 from the year before, compared with an increase of 4.4% to $1.42 billion for **computer games**, according to research firm NPD Group Inc. of Port Washington, N.Y."
Here was where I got the $9 billion figure. My memory was okay, but it didn't go far enough. The *Journal* did indeed say

something about a $9.4 billion industry, but it was referring to the *American* games industry, not the global one. Note that that figure referred to "videogames"—the author's term for console games—in contrast to "computer games." No wonder I was confused. Console games are a subset of computer games. However, note that neither the console figure nor the computer games total came anywhere close to the $6.35 billion reported by the IDSA. The mystery deepened.

The Second Article

This article provided the number of online gamers, but no dollar amounts for either online or other types of computer games.

The Third Article

The author must indeed have been defining the scope of the industry in a different way from the IDSA because he said that revenues for 2001 were expected to reach nearly $50 billion! Aha—I discovered that he was referring to global figures. Reading further, I saw that another reason for the high number was that the author was including mobile, interactive TV, arcades, rental games, and online games as well as the traditional PC and console sectors. No wonder the number was so high. But on further examination, I discovered a table at the end of the article that broke the number down by sector, and I could calculate that PC and console games together totaled $25 billion in 2001. That number was in line with the April 2002 article from the *Times of London*, which put the global industry at about $21 billion. The numbers here came from a U.K. firm, Informa Media Group PLC, which was not the same source the *Times* used. That meant that two sources were roughly in sync with each other. Hurray for our side.

I spent about $15 for this information and was still confused. I decided to go back to the IDSA and see if there was any information about its methodology.

There wasn't, but the association did list sources and something more. There was a chart on page 10 of the report that broke the number $6.35 billion down into videogames, computer games, and edutainment, and there was a concluding statement on the last page of the report that explained that the $6.35 billion was for *U.S.* sales. Okay, so was the $9.4 billion figure. So what was going on? One source said that the U.S. market was about $6 billion and another said it was about $9 billion. Were they using different methodology? Now it was hair-pulling time because both sources cited the same producer! The $9.4 billion came from NPD Group and the $6.35 billion from NPD FunWorld and NPD TechWorld.

At this point, it was probably time to call NPD to find out why the numbers were so different. In real life I would have done that. But for the sake of this case study, I decided to look online some more.

I decided to go to a games industry Web site: Gamasutra at http://www.gamasutra.com. There I discovered the following:

Video Games Sales to Top $31 Billion in 2002
The video games industry is on track for a record year in 2002, with global sales projected to increase by 12 percent to $31 billion, a new report by British research firm Informa Media Group said on Monday…Combined console and hardware sales will account for $22 billion, or nearly 70 percent of the market in 2002…Conversely, sales of PC games plus handheld games and hardware are showing signs of weakness. Groups' sales are expected to dip by a combined 8.5 percent to $8.5 billion this year…Meanwhile, sales in the nascent categories of online, mobile phone and interactive television games is expected to double this year to $873 million, Informa Media Group said.

This article seemed to have reasonable numbers in it. In 2001, the global computer games industry was in the low to mid 20 billions of dollars. To reach just about 30 billion in 2002 was not unreasonable. I was tempted to accept the two rough sets of figures for the global industry, broadly defined.

The prediction of a rise to $85 billion by 2006 was a bit of a stretch, particularly considering that the article claimed that $85 billion represented a 71% increase over the present total, which it didn't. As far as whether the U.S. games industry totals $6 billion or $9 billion, I was content to rack the variation up to a difference in the things being counted.

If I were doing this search for real, I would now start calling the sources and asking questions about methodology.

Lessons Learned

✔   Even when a source looks old, it can provide clues to other more recent sources.

✔   It is a good idea to exercise a little skepticism when figures don't look right to you.

✔   Be sure you know exactly what is being counted. Are the figures for one country, a region, the whole world? How is the thing being counted defined, and what does it include? Often you will have to dig to find out.

✔   Broaden searches that don't yield enough information. You can do that by changing vocabulary, publications or other sources searched, dates, or part of the document searched.

✔   Your memory can both fool and help you. Always verify what it is telling you.

✔   You may have to call sources on the phone to clarify the information you find online.

Chapter 5

U.S. Industry Sources

How Industry and General Business Data Are Gathered

Industry and business data come from the following sources:

- National statistical offices
- International statistical offices
- Government surveys
- Government publications
- Government administrative records
- Research and industry reports (consultants, scholars, private companies)
- Analyst (brokerages and financial firms) and bank reports
- News releases
- Trade journals
- Trade associations

Types of Data
Market Data

Current, historical, and forecast data all go into the pot of the market researcher, who may also stir in:

Measures of Market Size and Characteristics

- Market shares

- Market sizes

- Product segments

- Demand

- Sales (in dollars or other units of currency, per item, or in units of measure, such as tons, gallons, bushels, and so on). Sales can be used to rank the players and calculate market share. Sales figures are essential for tracking which kinds of products are selling, where, and to whom.

- Market growth or decline

- Types of producers (conglomerates, small specialty companies, etc.)

- Mergers and acquisitions

Financials

- Profits and losses

- Returns

- Prices

- Dollar amount of average, low, and high transactions

- Advertising prices and expenditures

- Financing, including government funding

- Labor costs, worker salaries and benefits costs, payrolls

- Imports/exports, tariffs

Innovation and Promotion

- New products (introductions)

- Advertising angles (such as companies that promote environmental benefits), channels

- Promotions

- Packaging

- Distribution channels

Customers

- Brand recognition
- Demographics of consumers and other buyers, purchasing patterns, customer loyalty
- Product successes and failures

Internal Operations

- Locations (domestic, foreign, by state or other geographic division)
- Numbers and types of employees
- Equipment use
- Capital and other expenditures (for example, for pollution control, transportation, insurance, and research and development)
- Raw materials and ingredients used
- Use of space and other resources

Other

- Trends in regulation
- Demographics and earnings and/or perks of CEOs, CFOs, and other company leaders and business owners

Industry Data

In addition to data on markets, researchers may add a cup or three of information about the entire industry, using additional ingredients such as:

- Production
- Productivity
- Insurance risk
- Leading industries per geographic area, nation, or world

Business Data

Finally, general business information seasons the brew, adding measures such as:

- Business failures

- Numbers of home-based businesses

- Numbers of telecommuters

- Numbers of consultants

- Businesses owned by women, minorities, and foreign-born people

Market Size

When people speak of market size, they mean one of two things: the total universe from which their market can be drawn, which is actually *potential* market size, and the number of actual purchases made or total revenue therefrom. The latter is more prevalent and more accurate. For example, if I say that the U.S. aerospace industry market size is $400 billion, that means that that much money is generated by the industry. However, if I say that my target market for my new software product is 5 million people, I mean the universe of potential buyers, not the number of people who actually purchase the product.

Market size is a useful measure of potential sales of products and services or to gauge the size of an industry in general, but unless it is carefully analyzed, it is only a ballpark figure.

General Sources

Bizjournals.com, http://www.bizjournals.com. Business news from 41 local U.S. markets and 46 industries. Also covers national news. Archives go back to 1996.

Business Week, http://www.businessweek.com. A fabulous source, but it is only available to subscribers unless you access it through aggregators like Factiva (www.factiva.com) and eLibrary (http://www.eLibrary.com).

Businesswire, http://www.businesswire.com. Press releases covering the last seven days. Company and industry information.

Factiva, http://www.factiva.com. $2.95 per article and a $69 per-year password fee.

FindArticles, http://www.FindArticles.com/PI/index.jhtml. Search and retrieve for free! Dates back to 1998.

Forbes, http://www.forbes.com

Fortune, http://www.fortune.com

International Trade Administration, http://www.ita.doc.gov

Los Angeles Times, http://www.latimes.com

The Paperboy, http://www.thepaperboy.com.au/welcome.html. Identify and go straight to newspapers around the world; search headlines of major news sources through one interface. Ridiculously inexpensive. There are world, U.K., and Canadian editions. $

Reed Business Information, http://www.reedbusiness.com. Publishes various journals.

Reuters, http://www.reuters.com. World news. Clumsy to search.

Service Annual Survey from the U.S. Bureau of the Census, http://www.census.gov/ftp/pub/econ/www/servmenu.html. Service industries: truck transportation, couriers and messengers, warehousing, information industries, publishing, motion pictures, sound recordings, broadcasting, telecommunications, data processing, securities and commodity contracts intermediation and brokerages, rental and leasing services, professional services, scientific and technical services, waste management, administration, healthcare, social assistance, arts, entertainment, recreation, sports, museums, amusement, gambling, repair and maintenance, personal services, religious services, civic organizations, grantmaking.

USA Today, http://www.usatoday.com/usafront.htm

The *Wall Street Journal* is a fabulous source of statistics! http://www.wsj.com $

Market Share
U.S. Business Reporter at http://www.activemediaguide. com/prospectus_cp.htm offers quick market share figures for a variety of U.S. industries.

Agriculture

AgWeb.com, http://www.dairytoday.com. Agriculture.

BEEF, http://www.beef-mag.com

Farm Industry News, http://www.farmindustrynews.com

U.S. Department of Agriculture National Agricultural Statistics Service, http://www.usda.gov/nass

U.S. Poultry & Egg Association, http://www.poultryegg.org

Energy, Minerals, and Metals

American Wind Energy Association, http://www.awea.org

Coal Age, http://www.coalage.com

Metal Industry Indicators from the U.S. Geological Survey, http://minerals.usgs.gov/minerals/pubs/mii

Platt's, http://www.platts.com. Energy around the world.

Platts Metals Week,
http://www.platts.com/plattsmetals/newsletters.shtml

Minerals Industry from the U.S. Geological Survey,
http://minerals.usgs.gov/minerals

Transmission & Distribution World, http://www.tdworld.com. Power transmission and distribution.

Utility Business, http://www.utilitybusiness.com. Power industry.

Advertising

AC Nielsen, http://www.acnielsen.com. Retail and media measurement. Includes box office and Internet. You can find some free information at the site. International. Some $

Advertiser, http://www.ana.net/advertiser/advertiser.htm. Published by the Association of National Advertisers. Information for advertisers. Demographics, attitudes, purchasing habits. Most information restricted to members. $

Advertising Age, http://www.adage.com. National advertisers, expenditures in newspapers, top 100 U.S. markets.

Adweek, http://www.adweek.com. Includes box office, music charts, concert grosses, most-played videos. Most other services cost $.

Adweek Magazines' Technology Marketing,
http://www.marketingcomputers.com/mc/index.jsp

American Business Media, http://www.americanbusinesspress.com. Ad pages.

Brandweek, http://www.adweek.com. Some free info. Most services cost $.

U.S. company that spends the most on media advertising: McDonald's $628,904,200 in 2002

Strategy: Search Brandweek on FindArticles.com using *media spending rank*.

Article title: "America's Top 2000 Brands." This roundup is published every June.

Cost: Free.

Note that in most cases, you can substitute Dow Jones for FindArticles. While the journals covered are not exactly the same, the type of content is similar. I fear that some day FindArticles may go away, but I can't see that happening with Factiva.

Cable TV Advertising Bureau, http://www.cabletvadbureau.com

Catalog Age Magazine, http://industryclick.com/magazine.asp?magazineid=153&siteid=2

Direct Marketing News, http://www.dmnews.com. Fee to purchase articles from the archive. $

Mediaweek, http://www.adweek.com. Market indicators, media market profiles, TV network market shares. Most services cost $.

Outdoor Advertising Association of America, http://www.oaaa.org

Point of Purchase Advertising International, http://www.popai.com

Promotional Products Association International, http://www.ppa.org

Promo, http://www.industryclick.com/magazine.asp?magazineid=122&SiteID=2. Promotional products.

Promotional Products Business, http://www.ppai.org/Publications/PPB

Response, http://www.responsemagazine.com. Television direct response.

Reed Business Information, http://www.reedbusiness.com

Apparel

Accessories, http://www.busjour.com. Women's fashion accessories.

Footwear News, http://www.footwearnews.com. Staff will do searches for you for a small fee. $

Stitches, http://industryclick.com/magazine.asp?siteid=25& magazineid=39. Commercial embroidery industry.

Wearables Business, http://www.wearablesbusiness.com. Promotional and corporate apparel.

Women's Wear Daily, http://www.wwd.com. Staff will do searches for you for a small fee. $

Number of people who belong to health clubs: About 33 million.

Source: *Club Industry* magazine.
Strategy: Search the magazine at http://www. clubindustry.com using the word *statistics*.
Cost: Free.

In an article entitled "The Changing Face of Fitness," it says that the senior market represents 22.5 percent of the 7.4 million U.S. club members. Do the math, and voilá! About 33 million total.

> **Online book sales in the first quarter of 2002 were $557 million.**
>
> **Source:** *Internet Business News*, M2 Communications Ltd.
> **Strategy:** FindArticles.com, *+online +book +sales +2002.*
>
> **Cost:** Free.
>
> **Article title:** "Sales from US Web sites increase in Q1 2002."

Broadcasting

BE Radio, http://industryclick.com/magazine.asp?magazineid=135&siteid=15. Broadcast engineering.

Broadcast Engineering, http://industryclick.com/magazine.asp?magazineid=158&siteid=15

Broadcasting & Cable, http://www.tvinsite.com. This site also lets you search TVInsite, Cablevision, Multichannel News, TVInsite International, Multichannel News International, Television Europe, and Television Latin America.

Cableworld, http://www.inside.com/default.asp?entity=CableWorld. $

Federal Communications Commission, http://www.fcc.gov. Select Media Bureau, then Industry Analysis Division, then Media Bureau Reports. Radio, television, cable, video. For wireless, select Wireless Telecommunications Bureau, then Releases, then WTB Reports.

Chemicals

American Plastics Council, http://www.plastics.org

Chemical Engineering, http://www.che.com. Reasonable prices. $

Chemical and Engineering News, http://pubs.acs.org/cen

Chemical News and Intelligence, http://www.cnionline.com. International. Some very good information is free here.

Chemical Week, http://www.chemweek.com

Modern Plastics, http://www.modplas.com. Some free. Very reasonable prices. $

The Society of the Plastics Industry, http://www.plasticsindustry.org

Construction

Cement Americas, http://www.cementamericas.com. Global cement industry.

Concrete Products, http://www.concreteproducts.com

Construction Equipment, http://www.constructionequipment.com

Engineering News-Record, http://enr.construction.com/Default.asp. Construction industry.

International Construction, http://www.intlconstruction.com

Pit & Quarry, http://www.pitandquarry.com/pitandquarry

Electronics

Access Control & Security Systems, http://industryclick.com/magazine.asp?magazineid=119&siteid=24. Security industry.

Clean Rooms, http://cr.pennnet.com/home.cfm. Contamination control.

Consumer Electronics Association, http://www.ebrain.org. Expensive, but often the best source. $

Electronic Business, http://www.e-insite.net/eb-mag. Electronics industry.

Laser Focus World, http://lfw.pennnet.com/home.cfm. Photonics and optoelectronics.

Semiconductor International, http://www.e-insite.net/semiconductor

Solid State Technology, http://sst.pennnet.com/home.cfm. International.

Entertainment

Amusement Business, http://www.amusementbusiness.com. Archived articles are inexpensive. $

BASELINE, http://baseline.hollywood.com. Box office grosses for the top films. Includes historical statistics.

Billboard, http://www.billboard.com. Music, video, home entertainment.

Computer Gaming World, http://www.gamers.com/cgw/index.jsp

Digital Media Net, http://www.digitalmedianet.com. Broadcast, animation, professional audio, postproduction, video, games.

Gama Network, http://www.gamasutra.com. Computer games.

Hollywood Reporter, http://www.hollywoodreporter.com. TV, music, media, film, Web. Relatively inexpensive. $

Interactive Digital Software Association, http://www.idsa.com/index.html. Video games, computer games, entertainment software.

International Game Developers Association, http://www.igda.org

Internet Movie Database, http://www.imdb.com

Playthings, http://www.playthings.com

Toy Industry Association, http://www.toy-tia.org/index.html

Variety, http://www.variety.com. Music, video, film, TV, Internet. Requires a subscription, but day and month passes are inexpensive. $

Budget for the movie *Being John Malkovich*: $13 million.

Source: Internet Movie Database, http://www.imdb.com.

Strategy: Searched on title. When I got to the page for the movie, clicked on link "Box Office & Business" in the navigation bar on the left.

Cost: Free.

Financial Services

ABA Banking Journal, http://www.banking.com/aba

American Bankers Association, http://www.aba.com/default.htm

The American Bankruptcy Institute, http://www.abiworld.org

American Financial Services Association, http://www.americanfinsvcs.org. See the publications.

The Banker, http://www.thebanker.com

FreeEdgar, http://www.freeedgar.com. SEC company filings.

Institutional Investor, http://www.institutionalinvestor.com

Insurance Information Institute, http://www.iii.org

Mortgage Bankers Association of America, http://www.mbaa.org

National Association of Realtors, http://www.realtor.org

National Real Estate Investor, http://industryclick.com/magazine.
asp?magazineid=126&siteid=23

National Venture Capital Association, http://www.nvca.org/
home-frame2.html

New York Stock Exchange, http://www.nyse.com

Risk & Insurance, http://www.riskandinsurance.com

Securities Industry Association, http://www.sia.com. They have
wonderful publications, but they aren't terribly cheap. Go to the
press area for free information.

Standard & Poor's, http://www.standardandpoors.com. Worldwide
investment vehicle ratings, economic analysis, and forecasts.

U.S. Banker, http://www.us-banker.com

U.S. Securities and Exchange Commission, http://www.sec.gov.
Securities markets, company filings.

**The vacancy rate for Atlanta office buildings 30,000
square feet and larger: 16.9 percent in the first quarter of
2002. For the same period the previous year, the vacancy
rate was 12.3 percent.**

Source: *Atlanta Business Chronicle*
Strategy: Went to http://www.bizjournals.com. Searched
last 60 days using *Atlanta office space.*
Cost: Free.

Food and Beverages

Beverage Digest, http://www.beverage-digest.com

Beverage World, http://www.beverageworld.com. For access to archives, you must pay by the month. $

Candy Industry, http://www.stagnito.com/default.asp

Confectioner, http://www.stagnito.com/default.asp

Dairy Field, http://www.stagnito.com/default.asp

Food Industry Research Center, http://www.grocerynetwork.com/ grocerynetwork/firc_new/index.jsp. Search the archives of Food Logistics, Food Service Director, Frozen Food Age, ID, Restaurant Business, Progressive Grocer, and Supermarket Business. Includes both print and online content. $

Frozen Food Age, http://www.frozenfoodage.com

InterBev, http://www.bevindustry.com. Beverage industry.

Meat Processing Magazine, http://www.meatnews.com. There are both North American and global editions.

Meat Processing News Online, http://www.meatnews.com

National Soft Drink Association, http://www.nsda.org

Private Label Magazine, http://www.privatelabelmag.com/index_ pop.htm

Quick Frozen Foods International, http://www.quickfrozenfoods.com

Refrigerated & Frozen Foods, http://www.stagnito.com/default.asp

Snack Food & Wholesale Bakery, http://www.stagnito.com/ default.asp

Snack Food Association, http://www.sfa.org/default.htm. See The Snack Report.

Wine Institute, http://www.wineinstitute.org

Winebusiness.com, http://www.winebusiness.com

U.S. Sales of California Table Wine in 2001

Source: Winebusiness.com

Strategy: Searched on *retail sales*.

Cost: Free.

Retail/750m	Revenue
Low (Under $8)	$2,548,063,028
Mid ($8–$15)	$1,570,667,563
High ($15+)	$2,169,552,282
Total All Wine	$6,288,282,872

Healthcare and Fitness

Club Industry, http://www.clubindustry.com. Fitness industry.

Consumer Healthcare Products Association, http://www.chpa-info.org

Drug Topics, http://www.drugtopics.com

IMS Health, http://www.ims-global.com. Healthcare and pharmaceuticals.

Medical Marketing & Media, http://www.cpsnet.com/Pubs/mmm. asp. Healthcare and pharmaceuticals.

Modern Healthcare, http://www.modernhealthcare.com

PhRMA (Pharmaceutical Research Companies), http://www.phrma.org

Biotechnology giant Amgen sold more than $2 billion worth of Epogen, its anti-anemia drug for patients on dialysis, in 2001. (The exact figure is $2,108,500,000.)

Source: Amgen's 2001 10-K filing dated February 26, 2002.

Strategy: I went to the NASDAQ Web site at http://www.nasdaq.com, entered Amgen's ticker symbol *AMGN* in the quote box, and clicked on Flash Quote. I then clicked on the link to the stock in the brief results, then Real-time Filings, then 10-K. The information about Amgen's flagship product appeared within the first few paragraphs, which explain the company's business.

Cost: Free.

Here's another way you can find the same information. Go to IMS Health at http://www.imshealth.com and select News Releases. (I checked this link because I know that drug rankings are released once a year by companies that track and publish them. That event always warrants a press release.) I read through the titles until I found something called "IMS reports 16.9 percent growth in 2001 U.S. prescription sales." This sounded like it could be the announcement I was looking for. If we know the total in prescription sales, we might know sales for major drugs as well. And in fact, there was a list of the Top 10 best sellers for 2001. Epogen was number 6 at $2.6 billion. Why the discrepancy between this report and that of the company? IMS Health explains that its data were gathered over 53 weeks rather than 52. Nevertheless, $500 million (the difference between the two figures) seems like a lot for one week. It is likely that the difference also reflects different counting methods.

Here's still another way: Search Google using *epogen sales 2002*. I used 2002 because 2001 sales would be announced in 2002. Had I not used that date, I would have retrieved a mountain of information that's too old. The third result was: Signals Magazine: Turn Signal - Solid Gold Sales 02/23/2002: "Aranesp, which requires less frequent dosing that Epogen, is prescribed ... or longer half-life, can also result in solid gold sales ... originally published 02/23/2002..."

Since the date of the article was 2002, I took a chance that there might be 2001 sales figures. Sure enough, there were. *Signals Magazine*, an online biotechnology magazine, is published by Recombinant Capital in Walnut Creek, California. The article includes a chart of established biotech drug sales in 2000 and 2001. Epogen sales were $1.96 billion in 2000 and $2.106 billion in 2001.

Information Technology and Communications

Baseline Magazine, http://www.baselinemag.com. Enterprise information technology.

BtoB, http://www.btobonline.com/webPriceIndex/index.html. Cost of developing a Web site in various markets.

CED, http://www.cedmagazine.com. Communications, including broadband, cable, fiber optics.

CIO, http://www.cio.com. Information technology.

CIO Insight, http://www.cioinsight.com. Information technology.

C/Net, http://www.cnet.com. Computing, communications, media, e-business, personal technology.

Computerworld, http://www.computerworld.com

CRN, http://www.crn.com. Computer hardware and software.

Enterprise Systems, http://www.esj.com. Information technology.

Eweek, http://www.eweek.com. E-business.

Federal Computer Week, http://www.federalcomputerweek.com. Federal information technology.

Global Telephony, http://industryclick.com/magazine.asp? magazineid=2&siteid=3

Lightwave, http://lw.pennnet.com/home.cfm. Fiber optic communications technologies worldwide.

Information Week, http://www.informationweek.com. Information technology.

InfoWorld, http://www.infoworld.com. Information technology.

The Internet Economy Indicators, http://www.internetindicators.com

Netcraft Web Server Surveys, http://www.netcraft.com/Survey/ Reports

Network Magazine, http://www.networkmagazine.com

NUA Internet Surveys, http://www.nua.ie/surveys

Satellite Broadband, http://industryclick.com/magazine.asp? MagazineID=5&SiteID=3

Telephony, http://industryclick.com/microsites/index.asp?pageid= 844&srid=10164&magazineid=7&siteid=3

VARBusiness, http://www.varbusiness.com. Digital "solutions."

Video Systems, http://www.industryclick.com/magazine.asp? magazineid=127&SiteID=15

Wireless Review, http://industryclick.com/magazine.asp? magazineid=9&siteid=3

Wireless Week, http://www.wirelessweek.com

ZDNet, http://www.zdnet.com. Computing in the U.S. and around the world.

Money lost to Internet fraud (2000 vs. 2001):
$3,387,530 vs. $4,371,724

Source: Ziff Davis Smart Business
Strategy: Went to Web site, searched on *Internet fraud*.
Cost: Free.

Manufacturing

Appliance Magazine, http://www.appliancemagazine.com. This site covers the U.S., but there are links to European and Latin American sites here.

Appliance Manufacturer, http://www.ammagazine.com

Control Engineering, http://www.manufacturing.net/ctl. Control, instrumentation, and automation systems worldwide.

Current Industrial Reports from the U.S. Census Bureau, http://www.census.gov/pub/cir/www/index.html

Economic Census Manufacturing Reports, http://www.census.gov/prod/www/abs/manu-min.html. Published every five years.

Grocery Manufacturers of America, http://www.gmabrands.com

Industry Week, http://www.industryweek.com. Manufacturing and supporting industries.

Manufacturing.net, http://www.manufacturing.net. Both U.S. and international.

Optoelectronics Manufacturing, http://om.pennnet.com/home.cfm. Opto-electronics and photonics manufacturing.

Publishing

American Booksellers Association, http://www.bookweb.org

American Business Press, http://www.americanbusinesspress.com. Includes readership and circulations of business publications.

American Library Association, http://www.ala.org. Libraries.

American Society of Composers, Authors and Publishers (ASCAP), http://www.ascap.com. Music royalties.

Association of American Publishers, http://www.publishers.org

Association of American University Presses, http://aaup. uchicago.edu. You will probably have to call.

Association of Free Community Papers, http://www.afcp.org

Audit Bureau of Circulation, http://www.accessabc.com. Circulation of newspapers and other periodicals.

Book Industry Study Group, http://www.bisg.org. Most info must be purchased in publication form, but some can be gleaned from press releases. $

BookWire, http://www.bookwire.com

Christian Retailing, http://www.christianretailing.com

Circulation Management, http://www.circman.com or http://www. industryclick.com/magazine.asp?magazineid=122&SiteID=2

Editor and Publisher, http://www.editorandpublisher.com. Newspaper industry in U.S. and Canada.

Evangelical Christian Publishers Association, http://www.ecpa.org

Graphic Arts Information Network, http://www.gain.org. Printing industry.

National Music Publishers Association, http://www.nmpa.org

Newspaper Association of America, http://www.naa.org

Publishers Marketing Association, http://www.pma-online.org. $

Publishers Weekly, http://publishersweekly.reviewsnews.com

Romance Writers of America, http://www.rwanational.org

Society for Scholarly Publishing, http://www.sspnet.org

Software Publishers Association, http://www.spa.org

Special Libraries Association, http://www.sla.org

Retail

Automatic Merchandiser, http://www.automaticmerchandiser.com. Vending machine industry.

Chain Store Age, http://www.chainstoreage.com

Children's Business, http://www.childrensbusiness.com. Staff will search on your behalf for a small fee. $

DSN Retailing Today, http://www.dsnretailingtoday.com

Drug Store News, http://www.drugstorenews.com. Archived articles are inexpensive. $

Furniture Today, http://www.furnituretoday.com

Gourmet Retailer, http://www.gourmetretailer.com

National Retail Federation, http://www.nrf.com. Some info costs $, but not all. $

National Retail Hardware Association, http://www.nrha.org

Nation's Restaurant News, http://www.nrn.com. Archived articles are inexpensive. $

Progressive Grocer, http://www.progressivegrocer.com

Restaurants and Institutions, http://www.rimag.com

Retail and Wholesale Trade, U.S. Census Bureau, http://www.census.gov/econ/www/retmenu.html

Retail Merchandiser, http://www.retail-merchandiser.com

Shopping Center World, http://www.scwonline.com

Stores Magazine, http://www.stores.org

Supermarket News, http://www.supermarketnews.com. Some info is free. You must be a subscriber to get into the archives. $

Space and Aerospace

Aerospace Industries Association, http://aia-aerospace.org

Office of Space Commercialization (U.S. Department of Commerce Technology Administration), http://www.ta.doc.gov/space. Space transportation, remote sensing, satellite communications, satellite navigation.

Satellite Industry Association, http://www.sia.org

Space News, http://www.space.com/spacenews. You must be a subscriber. $

Space.com, http://www.space.com

Transportation

Air Transport World, http://www.atwonline.com

Airport Business, http://www.airportbiz.com

American Association of Port Authorities, http://www.aapa-ports.org. Port industry in the Western Hemisphere.

American Public Transport Association. http://www.apta.com

Association of American Railroads, http://www.aar.org

AviationNow, http://www.aviationnow.com. Sponsored by Aviation Week & Space Technology. Covers commercial, business, and military aviation and space.

Bureau of Transportation Statistics, http://www.bts.gov

Federal Aviation Administration, http://nasdac.faa.gov

Insurance Institute for Highway Safety/Highway Loss Data Institute, http://www.carsafety.org

Intermodal Transportation Database, http://www.itdb.bts.gov. All kinds of transportation statistics.

The International Air Cargo Association, http://www.tiaca.org

International Air Transport Association, http://www1.iata.org/index.htm

Modern Tire Dealer, http://www.mtdealer.com

Motor Carrier Financial and Operational Statistics from the U.S. Bureau of Transportation Statistics, http://www.bts.gov/ntda/mcs. Bus and trucking companies.

Newport's Truckinginfo.com, http://www.truckinginfo.com

Railway Age, http://www.railwayage.com

Transport News, http://www.transportnews.com. All modes of transportation.

Transport Topics, http://www.ttnews.com

Truckload Carriers Association, http://www.truckload.org

U.S. Department of Transportation, http://www.dot.gov. Select DOT News for links to each agency within the department.

Ward's Auto World, http://industryclick.com/microsites/index.asp? srid=10250&magazineid=1004&siteid=26

Ward's Dealer Business, http://industryclick.com/microsites/index. asp?srid=10250&magazineid=1004&siteid=26. Auto dealers.

A red light camera costs about $50,000. Installation and sensors cost about $5,000 per intersection.

Source: Insurance Institute for Highway Safety/Highway Loss Data Institute, http://www.carsafety.org.
Strategy: Selected link IIHS Research by Topic, then Red Light Cameras.
Cost: Free.

Travel and Tourism

Hotel & Motel Management, http://www.hotelmotel.com

International Trade Association Office of Travel & Tourism Industries, http://tinet.ita.doc.gov/research/programs/basic/index. html

Lodging Hospitality Online, http://www.lhonline.com

Meetings Industry News, http://industryclick.com/magazine.asp? magazineid=289&siteid=28

Travel Industry Association of America, http://www.tia.org. Some information is available to members only.

World Tourism Organization, http://www.world-tourism.org. Some costs $.

Miscellaneous

American City & County, http://industryclick.com/magazine.asp? magazineid=115&siteid=17. Local government.

American Printer, http://www.americanprinter.com

Council of Logistics Management, http://www.clm1.org

Waste Age, http://www.wasteage.com. Waste disposal industry.

Extended Case Study: U.S. Chilled Juice Sales, Market Shares

Purpose: This case study demonstrates how to find market share for a product using a variety of sources, and how to extrapolate that information to determine the entire market size for that product. In addition, it shows how to derive your own figures from those at hand.

Sources: Factiva, company annual reports, Beverage Industry Web site, http://www.bevindustry.com.

To find market share for the companies that make chilled juices in the U.S., I decided to start with Factiva because its coverage is so broad.

Using the strategy *juice and market share*, I searched All Publications, the headline and lead paragraph only, and the current year. I discovered that as of June 2002, Tropicana held 36 percent of the market for chilled juice sales in the

U.S. My source was the *Sarasota Herald-Tribune* from June 27, 2002. The cost? $2.95.

This information was all well and good, but I was looking for market shares for all the companies that make juice, not just Tropicana. Tropicana is a subsidiary of Pepsico, a public company. I wondered whether Pepsico's 10-K might provide more information on the environment in which the company operates, possibly providing overall market size or even identifying competitors. I figured that my odds were less than 50:50. There was a good chance that in typical fashion, the subsidiary's information might be rolled in with that of the company as a whole, and I wouldn't be able to tell anything about Tropicana specifically.

However, when I looked at Pepsico's annual report on its Web site (similar to the 10-K, which is a government filing, but not the same), I found a pie chart showing market shares of Tropicana and its competitors that offer chilled juices and drinks in the supermarket retail sales channel. It told me:

Tropicana	37%
Minute Maid	18%
Florida's Natural	8%
Private Label	16%
Procter & Gamble	6%
Others	15%

This information was terrific, but it referred to only one sales channel: retail supermarkets. Another chart in the report told me that supermarkets represent but 65% of Tropicana's sales channels, the others being:

Mass merchandise/club/military/drug stores	16%
Foodservice	7%
Convenience/direct store delivery/dairy	12%

Therefore, in order to find market share for all sales channels, I needed to find out what's happening in these channels. The annual report didn't tell me.

The annual report did list top-selling refrigerated juice brands in U.S. supermarkets with sales in millions. This information helped me translate market share into dollar amounts. The figures were in the form of a bar chart, which meant that I had to guess at the exact amounts by looking at where the end of the bar fell. I came up with:

Tropicana Pure Premium Orange Juice	$1.4 billion
Minute Maid Orange Juice	$600 million
Sunny Delight Drink	$280 million
Florida's Natural Orange Juice	$280 million
Minute Maid Drink	$100 million
Dole Blend	$100 million
Tampico Drink	$100 million
Tropicana Season's Best	$50 million
Tropicana Pure Premium Grapefruit Juice	$50 million
Welch's Drink	$50 million

Again, this chart represented only one sales channel. Note that Dole is a Tropicana brand.

I calculated the percentages:

Tropicana Pure Premium Orange Juice	47%
Minute Maid Orange Juice	20%
Sunny Delight	9%
Florida's Natural	9%
Minute Maid Drink	3%
Dole Blend	3%
Tampico Drink	3%

Tropicana Season's Best	2%
Tropicana Pure Premium Grapefruit Juice	2%
Welch's Drink	2%

Tropicana showed a much higher share than the 37 percent it cited in its annual report. Why was that? It was because this list represented only the top selling brands, not the entire universe of chilled juices sold through supermarkets. Tropicana held 47 percent of the top brands, not of all of them. I couldn't blame Tropicana for attempting to fool people here. I was the one who took dollar amounts and converted them to percentages. Use such results with caution.

Pepsico's 2001 10-K, which offered more financial information than its annual report, provided net sales (about $4 billion) and operating profit ($530 million) for Gatorade/Tropicana North America. I was lucky. Not all 10-Ks give figures for subsidiaries.

Just for the sake of comparison, I wanted to see if other sources confirmed any of these figures, so I went to Beverage Industry at http://www.bevindustry.com and selected Food & Beverage Report, then Industry Overviews: Beverage Products. There I found a link to Top 10 Brands of Refrigerated Orange Juice. Orange juice isn't all refrigerated juices, but it's a start. It turned out that the chart was for U.S. supermarket sales for 52 weeks ending April 22, 2001, well before the date of Pepsi's figures. This is what the chart showed me:

Top 10 Brands of Refrigerated Orange Juice

	$ sales (in millions)	Dollar share
Tropicana Pure Premium	$1,208.00	39.30%
Private Label	$618.80	20.10%
Minute Maid Premium	$613.20	19.90%
Florida's Natural	$261.40	8.50%

Tropicana Season's Best	$87.40	2.80%
Citrus World Donald Duck	$23.20	0.80%
Florida's Natural Growers Pride	$20.50	0.70%
Deans	$17.20	0.60%
Tree Ripe	$16.60	0.50%
Pet	$11.50	0.40%
Category total*	$3,075.40	100%

*All brands, not just the top 10

How did these figures compare to Pepsico's from approximately March 2002? They were close. Tropicana seemed to have lost market share since they were published (about 42 percent down to 37 percent). So had Minute Maid (20 percent down to 18 percent). Florida's Natural was about the same (8.5 percent to 8 percent). Procter & Gamble, with its Sunny Delight brand, didn't even appear on the Beverage Industry list, while Pepsico gave it a 6 percent share. Welch's was also absent from the Beverage Industry list. Was it possible that these brands gained a lot of market share since Beverage Industry compiled its list? It was, but that wasn't the issue: neither Sunny Delight nor Welch's is orange juice!

Now we come to an interesting question: Are Sunny Delight and Welch's competitors to Tropicana even though they aren't orange juice? The Beverage Industry list ignores them. But Pepsico obviously considers them competition, paying close attention to any company that makes refrigerated juice drinks. Could you broaden the definition of Tropicana's competition to include other kinds of cold drinks? The answer to that question is complex, but if you were writing a business plan for Tropicana, you'd want to look carefully at target markets, sales channels, and marketing strategies as well as other ways of quenching thirst in the first place (drinking fountains, for example).

How much did all this information cost me? A mere $3.

Neither the Pepsico annual report nor the Beverage Industry overview offered a total market size in dollars, though the latter mentioned that the total market for shelf-stable bottled juices was nearly $4 billion. However, if we wanted to know the total market size, we could calculate it based on the information we already retrieved.

The Sarasota paper said that Tropicana's share of the chilled juice market in the U.S. was 36 percent. The Pepsico annual report gave us further information. If we added up the dollar amounts of the top-selling Tropicana chilled juices in U.S. supermarkets, we would get $1.6 billion. (That's Tropicana and Dole.) However, we knew that that amount was for sales in supermarkets only and that supermarkets represented 65 percent of Tropicana's U.S. juice sales. Doing the math (divide $1.6 billion by .65), we could see that Tropicana's total U.S. juice sales came to $2.46 billion, representing 36 percent of the market. Again doing the math ($2.46 billion divided by .36), we could determine that the total U.S. chilled juice sale market came to about $6.8 billion, a little more than twice the total of the best-selling chilled juice brands and/or the chilled orange juice market.

Lessons Learned

✔   You can derive your own detailed figures from other people's general ones.

✔   You need to pay close attention to what the figures represent. For example, when looking at a company's market share or revenues, do not mistake numbers from one sales channel for the whole picture.

✔   Annual reports can provide a good overview of an industry as well as a particular company.

✔   Verify and extend the information you have by consulting multiple sources.

✔   Make sure you compare apples to apples. "Chilled juices" are not the same as "orange juice."

✔   You can find valuable information for very little money.

Chapter 6

Non-U.S. Industry Sources

The sources in this chapter cover a variety of industries in non-U.S. countries, with the emphasis on Australia, Canada, the U.K., Northern Ireland, Ireland, and New Zealand. You will also find general sources that cover Europe as well as government statistical agencies and central banks throughout the world. World sources are those that include information for the world as a whole and/or multiple countries. Dig in!

For a brief overview of how industry data are gathered and the types of information you can find, refer to Chapter 5, U.S. Industry Sources.

Australia
General

> Australia National Office for the Information Economy, http://itt. dcita.gov.au
>
> Australian Bureau of Statistics, http://www.abs.gov.au/Ausstats/abs @.nsf/ausstatshome. Population, trade, finance, labor, industrial production, telecommunications, information technology, major industries, motor vehicle registrations, etc.
>
> *Australian Financial Review*, http://afr.com. $
>
> Australian Government Industry Research & Analysis, http://www. industry.gov.au. Covers a wide range of industries.

Committee for Economic Development of Australia, http://www.ceda.com.au. The Australian economy from soup to nuts.

The Melbourne Age, http://www.quattro.com/id258.htm. Reasonable prices. $

Newstext.com.au, http://www.newstext.com.au/pages/main.asp. Covers national, regional, and local Australian and New Zealand newspapers. Reasonably priced. $

South China Morning Post, http://www.scmp.com. $

The Sydney Morning Herald, http://www.quattro.com/id263.htm. Reasonable prices. $

Agriculture, Environment, and Natural Resources

Australian Bureau of Agricultural and Resource Economics (ABARE), http://www.abareconomics.com. Agriculture, climate change, energy, minerals, trade, fisheries, natural resources.

Australian Dairy Corporation (ADC), http://www.dairycorp.com.au

Energy, Minerals, and Metals

Association of Mining & Exploration Companies, http://www.amec.asn.au

Financial Services

Reserve Bank of Australia, http://www.rba.gov.au/Statistics. Consumer price index, exchange rates, international reserves, credit cards, assets and liabilities of financial institutions, bank lending to business, etc.

Healthcare and Fitness

Biotechnology Australia, http://www.biotechnology.gov.au

Publicly listed core biotechnology companies, of which there are 35, spent about A$112 million on R&D, on average about A$3.2 million per annum each for the period mid-1999 to the end of 2001.

By comparison private and unlisted core biotechnology companies, of which there are 155, spent about A$1 million per annum each on R&D.

Source: Biotechnology Australia, Australian Biotechnology Report 2001.

Strategy: Went to http://www.biotechnology.gov.au, selected Industry & Research, then Reports, then *Australian Biotechnology Report 2001.*

Cost: Free.

Media, Publishing, Printing, and Broadcasting

Australian Book Web, http://www.books.aus.net/index.htm

Transportation

Motor Trades Association of Australia (MTAA), http://www.mtaa.com.au. Motor vehicle sales and registrations.

Travel and Tourism

Australian Bureau of Tourism Research, http://www.btr.gov.au

Miscellaneous

Australia TradeCoast, http://www.australiatradecoast.com.au. Port of Brisbane statistics.

Canada
General

Canadian Chamber of Commerce, http://www.chamber.ca/new pages/main.html. Covers a variety of industries and economic issues, including biotechnology, the economics of climate change, air travel, and so on.

Canadian Commercial Corporation, http://www.ccc.ca/eng/abo_ main.cfm. Transportation, aerospace, defense, information and communication technologies, electrical power equipment, major capital projects.

Department of Foreign Affairs and International Trade, http://www. infoexport.gc.ca. Market reports for a variety of industries and countries. Accessible to Canadians only.

Electric Library Canada, http://www.elibrary.ca. $

Financial Post, http://www.nationalpost.com/financialpost

GDSourcing Research and Retrieval, http://www.gdsourcing.com. Huge Canadian statistics metasite from a business research firm. You can purchase a reasonably priced guide for small business research as well.

Industry Canada, http://www.strategis.ic.gc.ca. Industry, economic, and trade statistics.

Industry Canada, Business Information by Sector, http://strategis. ic.gc.ca/sc _indps/engdoc/homepage.html. Includes not only Canada, but also the U.S. and Mexico. Covers a variety of industries, such as franchising, e-commerce, tourism, sporting goods, and so on.

Industry Canada Trade Data Online, http://strategis.ic.gc.ca/sc_mrkti/tdst/engdoc/tr_homep.html

Marketing Magazine, http://www.marketingmag.ca/index.cgi. Market shares for the packaged goods, retail, financial services, communications, and automotive industries are free. Archived articles are reasonably priced. $

Statistics Canada, http://www.statcan.ca/start.html

Strategis, http://strategis.ic.gc.ca/engdoc/main.html. Trade, investment, business information by sector, economic analysis. This is a general business and consumer portal with numerous helpful sections.

Agriculture, Environment, and Natural Resources

Agri-Food Trade Service, http://atn-riae.agr.ca. International trade and market information for Canadian agri-food exporters. Covers the world.

AgriWeb (Agriculture and Agri-food Canada), http://hahtext.agr.ca/agriweb/html/whatis-e.htm

Canadian Commercial Corporation, Environmental Technologies, http://www.ccc.ca/eng/abo_main.cfm

Fisheries and Oceans Canada, http://www.ncr.dfo.ca/home-accueil_e.htm. Ocean industries.

Forest Products Association of Canada, http://www.cppa.org/index.htm

Natural Resources Canada, http://mmsd1.mms.nrcan.gc.ca/forest/default_e.asp. Forestry.

Ontario Ministry of Agriculture and Food, http://www.gov.on.ca/
OMAFRA/english/food/export/index.html

Trade Team Canada, Agriculture, Food and Beverages, http://
ats-sea.agr.ca/info/can/e3204.htm

Chemicals

Industry Canada, Plastics, http://strategis.ic.gc.ca/sc_indps/sectors/
engdoc/plas_hpg.html. Includes plastics statistics for a few other
countries as well as for Canada.

Energy, Minerals, and Metals

Canadian Mining Journal, http://www.canadianminingjournal.com

The Mining Association of Canada, http://www.mining.ca. Includes
environmental statistics.

Financial Services

Canada Mortgage and Housing Corporation, http://www.
cmhc-schl.gc.ca/en/homadoin/excaprex/index.cfm

Department of Finance Canada, http://www.fin.gc.ca/fin-eng.html.
Budget, financial institutions and markets, economic and fiscal
information, social services.

Insurance Bureau of Canada, http://www.ibc.ca

Healthcare and Fitness

Health Canada, http://www.hc-sc.gc.ca/medicare. Healthcare insurance.

Industry Canada Biotechnology Gateway, http://strategis.ic.gc.ca/
SSG/bo01374e.html

Information Technology and Communications

Information Technology Association of Canada, http://www.itac.ca. See the annual review.

Manufacturing

Canadian Manufacturers and Exporters, http://www.the-alliance.org/ home. asp?l=EN&div=NAT

Media, Publishing, and Broadcasting

AC Nielsen Canada, http://www.acnielsen.ca. Retail market measurement.

Broadcaster Magazine, http://www.broadcastermagazine.com

Bureau of Broadcast Measurement, http://www.bbm.ca. Radio and television metrics.

Canadian Publishers' Council, http://www.pubcouncil.ca/home.htm. You will probably have to call.

Space and Aerospace

Aerospace Industries Association of Canada, http://www.aiac.ca

Canadian Commercial Corporation, Aerospace and Defence, http:// www.ccc.ca/eng/abo_main.cfm

Transportation

Transport Canada, http://www.tc.gc.ca/en/menu.htm

New Zealand
General

Business Demographics from Statistics New Zealand, http://www. stats.govt.nz/domino/external/web/prod_serv.nsf/htmldocs/Business +Demographics. People and households, business and economy.

Business Outlook from the National Bank of New Zealand, http:// www.nbnz.co.nz/economics/outlook/default.htm

Country reports from ECNext, http://www.ecnext.com. $

Industry New Zealand, http://www.industrynz.govt.nz. Biotechnology, creative industries, food, information and communications technology, niche manufacturing, wood processing, textiles.

Industry Sectors in New Zealand from the New Zealand Business Migrant Liaison Unit, http://www.business-migrants.govt.nz/Bml/ away/links/links-industry-sectors-01.htm. Many different industries.

Kiwi Careers, New Zealand, http://www.kiwicareers.co. nz/index.htm. Industry overviews.

The New Zealand Herald, http://www.nzherald.co.nz

New Zealand Industry Sector Analysis Reports from the U.S. Department of Commerce, http://tradeport.org/ts/countries/new zealand/isa/index.html. Various industries in New Zealand.

New Zealand Institute of Economic Research, http://www.nzier.org. nz. Economic analysis and forecasting, including specific industries.

New Zealand Market Research Reports from the U.S. Department of Commerce, http://tradeport.org/ts/countries/newzealand/mrr/ index.html

New Zealand Ministry of Economic Development, http://www. med.govt.nz/index.html. Information technology, e-commerce, tourism, energy.

New Zealand Ministry of Foreign Affairs and Trade, http://www.
mfat.govt.nz. Trade statistics.

Newstext.com.au, http://www.newstext.com.au/pages/main.asp.
Covers national, regional, and local Australian and New Zealand
newspapers. Reasonably priced. $

Otago Daily Times, http://www.odt.co.nz

South China Morning Post, http://www.scmp.com. $

Statistical Sources: New Zealand from the University of Auckland
Library, http://www2.auckland.ac.nz/lbr/stats/nz_pacific/NZsources.
htm

Statistics New Zealand, http://www.stats.govt.nz

Trade New Zealand, http://www.tradenz.govt.nz. Export statistics, industry profiles. See "Exporter essentials" and "Importer
essentials."

Trade Newsletters from ECNext, http://www.ecnext.com. Individual
articles are reasonably priced. $

Agriculture, Environment, and Natural Resources

New Zealand Forest Industries Magazine, http://www.nzforest.co.nz

New Zealand Ministry of Economic Development, Minerals,
http://www.med.govt.nz/crown_minerals/minerals/index.asp

Chemicals

Plastics New Zealand, http://www.plastics.org.nz

Financial Services

Global Register, http://www.globalregister.co.nz/prices.htm. New Zealand and Australia securities prices.

New Zealand Unlisted Securities from Direct Broking Ltd., http://www.directbroking.co.nz. Select Sharemarkets, then Security Tables.

Reserve Bank of New Zealand, http://www.rbnz.govt.nz. Incomes, prices.

WestpacTrust (New Zealand), http://www.westpactrust.co.nz. Consumer confidence, economic indicators, saving and investment.

Travel and Tourism

New Zealand Ministry of Tourism, http://www.tourism.govt.nz

Tourism Industry Association New Zealand, http://www.tianz.org.nz

Tourism New Zealand, http://www.tourisminfo.govt.nz/cir_home/index.cfm

United Kingdom and Northern Ireland
General

Business Startups and Closures: VAT Registrations and Deregistrations in the U.K., http://www.sbs.gov.uk

CAIN (Conflict Archive on the Internet), http://cain.ulst.ac.uk. Statistics having to do with "The troubles" and Northern Ireland in general.

Clearly Business, http://www.clearlybusiness.co.uk. U.K. market capsules and profiles from Datamonitor.

The Daily Telegraph, http://www.telegraph.co.uk

Financial Times, http://www.ft.com. In addition to the paper itself, you can subscribe to its world press monitor. $

The Guardian, http://www.guardian.co.uk. U.K. newspaper.

HBOS Plc. (Halifax Group and the Bank of Scotland), http://www.hbosplc.com/view/economicview.asp. U.K. economic outlook.

Institute for Social and Economic Research, http://www.iser.essex.ac.uk

National Statistics (U.K.), http://www.statistics.gov.uk. U.K. government official statistics site.

Nomis, http://www.nomisweb.co.uk. Official U.K., labour market statistics.

The Northern Ireland Executive, http://www.nics.gov.uk. Web site for the government of Northern Ireland. Includes agriculture and rural development, culture/arts/leisure, education, employment, enterprise, trade, investment, environment, finance, health and social services, regional and social development.

Northern Ireland Statistics and Research Agency (NISRA), http://www.nisra.gov.uk. Official Northern Ireland statistics.

The Scotsman, http://www.scotsman.com

Small and Medium Enterprises Statistics for the U.K., http://www.sbs.gov.uk

Small Business Enterprise in U.K. Disadvantaged Communities, http://www.sbs.gov.uk

Survival Rates for Small Firms in the U.K., http://www.sbs.gov.uk

Think Small First Indicators, http://www.sbs.gov.uk. Measures indicating suitability of the U.K. for small business.

The Times, http://www.the-times.co.uk. Reasonable prices. $

Trade Association Forum (U.K.), http://www.taforum.org. U.K. trade association locator.

Trade Partners U.K., http://www.tradepartners.gov.uk. Overviews of industries and countries for businesses that want to export from and invest in the U.K.

U.K. Department of Trade and Industry, http://www.dti.gov.uk. Huge number of resources and statistics on a variety of industries.

U.K. HM Customs and Excise, http://www.uktradeinfo.com

U.K. Online, http://www.ukonline.gov.uk. Gateway to U.K. government Web sites.

U.K. Skillsbase Labour Market Information Database, http://www. skillsbase.dfes.gov.uk. Projections, earnings, key skills, replacement demands, unemployment and vacancies, qualifications, etc.

Workthing, http://www.workthing.com. Salary checker for U.K. jobs. Gives average and highest salary for particular jobs if you select Salary Checker under the At Work tab.

Advertising, Media, Publishing, Printing, and Broadcasting

AC Nielsen, https://www.acnielsen.co.uk. Marketplace research.

Advertising Association, http://www.adassoc.org.uk

Audit Bureau of Circulations Ltd., http://www.abc.org.uk. Independently audited data in Internet traffic, newspaper and magazine circulation, and exhibition attendance measurement in the U.K. and Ireland.

TheBookseller.com, http://www.thebookseller.co.uk

BookTrack, http://www.booktrack.co.uk. Publisher market share, sales by genre, discount analysis, sales by region.

British Printing Industries Federation, http://www.bpif.org.uk

Call Centre Association (CCA), http://www.cca.org.uk

Department of Trade & Industry Statistics Directorate, http://www.dti.gov.uk. Regional and business competitiveness, insolvencies.

Direct Mail Information Service (DMIS), http://www.dmis.co.uk. Covers the U.K. and Europe.

Direct Selling Association (DSA), http://www.dsa.org.uk

Internet Advertising Bureau, U.K. (IAB), http://www.iabuk.net. Interactive advertising, e-commerce, online marketing.

JICREG (Joint Industry Committee for Regional Press Research), http://www.jicreg.co.uk. British newspaper readership and demographic data.

The Newspaper Industry (International Newspaper Marketing Association), http://www.newspaper-industry.org. International.

Newspaper Society (NS), http://www.newspapersoc.org.uk

Outdoor Advertising Association of Great Britain, http://www.oaa.org.uk

Periodical Publishers Association (PPA), http://www.ppa.co.uk

The Publishers Association, http://www.publishers.org.uk

Radio Advertising Bureau (RAB) (U.K.), http://www.rab.co.uk

Radio Joint Audience Research Limited (RAJAR), http://www.rajar.co.uk. Radio audiences.

Royal Mail (RM), http://www.royalmail.com. Reports on how various industries use direct mail in their marketing.

Scottish Newspaper Publishers Association (SNPA), http://www.snpa.org.uk

World Advertising Research Centre (WARC), http://www.warc.com. Economic data, ad spending for various countries (includes historic and forecasts), demographics. Some info is free.

The *Norwich Advertiser* has the highest circulation (number of copies sold/distributed) of any newspaper in the county of Norfolk, U.K., at 78,093. The North Norfolk News reaches the highest number of readers per copy sold or distributed: 3.3. Adults in Norfolk read the Norfolk Eastern Daily Press more than any other local or regional paper: 179,361.

Source: JICREG, The Joint Industry Committee for Regional Press Research

Strategy: Went to http://www.jicreg.co.uk, selected Readership Data, then Standard Reports. Selected county, then Norfolk.

Cost: Free.

Agriculture, Environment, and Natural Resources

Department for Environment, Food & Rural Affairs, http://www. defra.gov.uk/defrahome.asp. Food, farming, fishing, forestry.

Meat and Livestock Commission, http://v2.mlc.org.uk

Apparel

British Footwear Association, http://www.britfoot.com

Construction

Department of Trade and Industry Construction Directorate, http://www.dti.gov.uk/construction

The House Builders Federation, http://www.hbf.co.uk

Office of the Deputy Prime Minister, Housing Statistics, http://www.housing.odpm.gov.uk/research/hss/index.htm

Office of the Deputy Prime Minister, Planning Statistics, http://www.planning.odpm.gov.uk/stats.htm

Energy, Minerals, and Metals

Aluminium Federation, http://www.alfed.org.uk

Department of Trade and Industry Oil & Gas Directorate, http://www.og.dti.gov.uk

Electricity Association, http://www.electricity.org.uk

U.K. Petroleum Industry Association, http://www.ukpia.com

Entertainment

British Actors Equity Association, http://www.equity.org.uk. Pay rates.

British Video Association, http://www.bva.org.uk

Institute of Leisure & Amenity Management, http://www.ilam.co.uk. Magazine has useful information, but it is not online. You will need to phone.

Financial Services

Ample, http://www.iii.co.uk. U.K. investment information.

The Association of British Insurers, http://www.abi.org.uk

The Bank of England, http://www.bankofengland.co.uk

British Bankers Association, http://www.bba.org.uk

The Chartered Insurance Institute, http://www.cii.co.uk. Use the search function.

Council of Mortgage Lenders, http://www.cml.org.uk

First Trust Bank, http://www.ftbni.com. Economic and financial statistics for Northern Ireland.

HM Treasury, http://www.hm-treasury.gov.uk. U.K. government budget and economic data.

Inland Revenue, http://www.inlandrevenue.gov.uk. U.K. tax statistics.

Institute for Fiscal Studies, http://www.ifs.org.uk. Effect of U.K. fiscal policy and taxation on the economy and population.

U.K. Department of Finance and Personnel, http://www.dfpni. gov.uk/economics_division/index.htm. Quarterly economic report on Northern Ireland.

Percentage of the U.K. population that purchases private medical insurance: 9 percent.

Source: The Association of British Insurers, http://www. abi.org.uk

Strategy: Went to Web site, selected link "The U.K. insurance industry," then "Key Facts."

Cost: Free.

Food and Beverages

The British Beer & Pub Association, http://www.beerandpub.com

British Frozen Food Federation, http://www.bfff.co.uk

Chilled Food Association, http://www.chilledfood.org

Food & Drink Federation, http://www.fdf.org.uk

The Gin & Vodka Association of GB, http://www.ginvodka.org

Institute of Grocery Distribution, http://www.igd.org.uk

The Scotch Whisky Association, http://www.scotch-whisky.org.uk

Wine & Spirit Association of Great Britain/Northern Ireland, http://www.wsa.org.uk

Healthcare and Fitness

Association of the British Pharmaceutical Industry, http://www.abpi. org.uk

Bioindustry Association, http://www.bioindustry.org. Biotechnology.

Information Technology and Communications

Department of Trade and Industry Communications and Information Industries Directorate, http://www.dti.gov.uk/cii/services/ contentindustry/index.shtml. Publishing, information, Internet commerce, digital content, computer games, leisure software, broadband.

Office of the e-Envoy, Market Analysis, http://www.e-envoy.gov.uk/ estatmap/estatmap.htm. Internet and computer usage, broadband availability and costs, IT literacy, etc.

OFTEL U.K. Office of Telecommunications, http://www.oftel. gov.uk

Manufacturing

British Aerosol Manufacturing Association, http://www.bama.co.uk

British Furniture Manufacturers Association, http://www.bfm.org.uk

Tobacco Manufacturers' Association, http://www.the-tma.org.uk

Retail

Association of Convenience Stores, http://www.thelocalshop.com/tls/index.asp

British Association of Toy Retailers, http://www.batr.co.uk/batr2k/main.htm

British Retail Consortium, http://www.brc.org.uk

The Restaurant Association, http://www.ragb.co.uk

Space and Aerospace

British National Space Centre, http://www.bnsc.gov.uk

Society of British Aerospace Companies, http://www.sbac.co.uk

Transportation

British Marine Industries Federation, http://www.bmif.co.uk

Civil Aviation Authority, http://www.caa.co.uk

Department for Transport, http://www.transtat.dft.gov.uk

Retail Motor Industry Federation, http://www.rmif.co.uk

The Society of Motor Manufacturers & Traders (SMMT), http://www.smmt.co.uk

U.K. Auto Industry, http://www.autoindustry.co.uk/index.asp. Covers the U.K., Europe, and the world.

Travel and Tourism

Association of Exhibition Organisers, http://www.aeo.org.uk

British Tourist Authority, http://www.britishtouristauthority.org

Northern Ireland Tourist Board, http://www.nitb.com

Northern Ireland's Tourism and Business Information Site from the University of Ulster, http://www.busmgt.ulst.ac.uk/leisure/nitfacts/index.html

Star U.K., http://www.staruk.org.uk. Tourism.

Wales Tourist Board, http://www.wtbonline.gov.uk

Miscellaneous

British Security Industry Association, http://www.bsia.co.uk

Office of the Deputy Prime Minister, Fire Statistics, http://www.odpm.gov.uk/safety/fire/rds/index.htm

Office of the Deputy Prime Minister, Local Government Finance Statistics, http://www.local.dtlr.gov.uk/finance/stats/index.htm

The Pulp & Paper Information Centre, http://www.ppic.org.uk

Ireland
General

Central Bank of Ireland, http://www.centralbank.ie

Central Statistics Office Ireland, http://www.cso.ie

Dublin Chamber of Commerce, http://www.dubchamber.ie. Dublin statistics, plus links to national sources.

The Economist, http://www.economist.com. $

Irish Business and Employers Confederation, http://www.ibec.ie/ ibec/internet.nsf/LookupPageLink/IBEC_Opening

Irish Independent, http://www.unison.ie/irish_independent

The Irish Times, http://www.ireland.com. $

NiceOne.com, http://www.niceone.com. Irish Internet portal. See Business & Finance, Info & Resources.

On Business, http://www.onbusiness.ie/ndm. Enterprise Ireland's compilation of major Irish financial and economic statistics.

Regional Media Bureau of Ireland, http://www.unison.ie/allpapers. php3. Links to regional newspapers.

Small Firms Association (Ireland), http://www.sfa.ie. Surveys on issues that affect small business.

The Sunday Business Post, http://www.sbpost.ie

The Times and *The Sunday Times*, http://www.the-times.co.uk. Reasonable prices. $

Chemicals

The Irish Pharmaceutical & Chemical Manufacturers Federation, http://www.ibec.ie/ibec/internet.nsf/LookupPageLink/IPCMFWebsite

Construction

Building Materials Federation, http://www.ibec.ie/ibec/internet.nsf/ LookupPageLink/BMFWebsite

Entertainment

Audiovisual Federation, http://www.ibec.ie/ibec/buspolicies/buspoliciesdoclib3.nsf/webPages/Audiovisual_Federation?OpenDocument

Financial Services

Central Bank of Ireland, http://www.centralbank.ie

Department of Finance of the Government of Ireland, http://www.irlgov.ie/finance/defaultbody.htm. Budgetary and economic statistics.

Financial Services Industry Association, http://www.ibec.ie/ibec/internet.nsf/LookupPageLink/FSIAWebsite

FinFacts Irish Finance Portal, http://www.finfacts.com. Securities markets, salary surveys, company rankings, economy.

Irish Government Department of Finance, http://www.irlgov.ie/finance/defaultbody.htm

Johnbeggs.com, http://www.johnbeggs.com/jb/default.asp. Economy and finance.

Information Technology and Communications

Integrated Technology Web, The Portal for Ireland, http://www.itw.ie. Gateway to trade shows and sources of information.

Technology Ireland, http://www.technologyireland.ie. See the yearbook for industry overviews. $

TIU TechWatch, http://www.techwatch.ie. Irish technology statistics. See the feature articles.

Media, Publishing, Printing, and Broadcasting

AC Nielsen of Ireland, http://acnielsen.com/ie. Retail and entertainment measurement.

Audit Bureau of Circulations Ltd., http://www.abc.org.uk. Independently audited data in Internet traffic, newspaper and magazine circulation, and exhibition attendance measurement in the U.K. and Ireland.

Travel and Tourism

Irish Tourist Board, http://www.ireland.travel.ie/home/index.asp. Tourism in Ireland.

Africa

Algeria. Statistics Algeria, http://www.ons.dz

South Africa. Statistics South Africa, http://www. statssa.gov.za/default3.asp

South African Reserve Bank, http://www.reservebank.co.za

Asia and the Pacific

Asian Development Bank, http://www.adb.org

Association of Southeast Asian Nations (Asean), http://www. aseansec.org. Macroeconomic indicators, trade, transportation, telecommunications, tourism.

Forbes Asian edition, http://www.forbes.com/home_asia

The South China Morning Post, http://www.scmp.com. Covers all of Asia plus Australia and New Zealand. $

United Nations Economic and Social Commission for Asia and the Pacific, http://www.unescap.org

Bangladesh. Bureau of Statistics, http://www.bbsgov.org

Cambodia. National Institute of Statistics, http://www.nis.gov.kh

China. National Bureau of Statistics of China, http://www.stats.gov.cn

Fiji Islands. Fiji Islands Statistics Bureau, http://www.statsfiji.gov.fj

Hong Kong. Business-Stat Online, http://stat.tdc.org.hk

Hong Kong Census and Statistics Department, http://www.info.gov.hk/censtatd

India. Ministry of Finance, Government of India, http://finmin.nic.in/index.html. See especially the economic survey.

Reserve Bank of India, http://www.rbi.org.in/hindi/index.html

Indonesia. Bank Indonesia, http://www.bi.go.id/bank_indonesia2

Statistics Indonesia, http://www.bps.go.id/index.shtml

Japan. Bank of Japan, http://www.boj.or.jp

Japan Information Network, http://www.jinjapan.org

Japan Institute for Social and Economic Affairs, http://www.kkc.or.jp/english/index.html

Japan Ministry of Economy, Trade and Industry, http://www.meti.go.jp/english/statistics/h_main.html

Japan Ministry of Finance, http://www.mof.go.jp/english/index.htm

Japan Statistics Bureau and Statistics Centre, http://www.stat.go.jp

Korea. Bank of Korea, http://www.bok.or.kr

Korea National Statistical Office, http://www.nso.go.kr

Malaysia. Central Bank of Malaysia, http://www.bnm.gov.my http://www.bnm.org/

Department of Statistics Malaysia, http://www.statistics.gov.my

Mongolia. National Statistical Office of Mongolia, http://nso.mn

Philippines. Central Bank of the Philippines, http://www.bsp.gov.ph

National Statistical Coordination Board, Philippines, http://www.nscb.gov.ph

National Statistics Office, Republic of the Philippines, http://www.census.gov.ph

Singapore. Monetary Authority of Singapore, http://www.mas.gov.sg

Statistics Singapore, http://www.singstat.gov.sg

Sri Lanka. Department of Census and Statistics, Sri Lanka, http://www.statistics.gov.lk

Taiwan. Taiwan Trade, http://www.taiwantrade.com.tw. Reasonable prices. $

Thailand. Bank of Thailand, http://www.bot.or.th/bothomepage/ index/index.asp or http://www.tcmb.gov.tr

National Statistical Office, Thailand, http://www.nso.go.th

Vietnam. Vietnam National Administration of Tourism, http://www. vietnamtourism.com

Eastern Europe, Russia, and the Commonwealth of Independent States

Armenia. Central Bank of Armenia, http://www.cba.am

National Statistical Service of the Republic of Armenia, http://www.armstat.am

Azerbaijan. State Statistical Committee of Azerbaijan Republic, http://www.statcom.baku-az.com

Belarus. Ministry of Statistics and Analysis of the Republic of Belarus, http://www.president.gov.by/Minstat/en/main.html

Bosnia-Herzegovina. Centralna Banka Bosne I Hercegovine (Central Bank of Bosnia Herzegovina), http://www.cbbh.gov.ba/en/index.html

Bulgaria. National Statistical Institute of the Republic of Bulgaria, http://www.nsi.bg

Bulgarian National Bank, http://www.bnb.bg

CIS. Business Information for the Newly Independent States (BIS-NIS), http://www.bisnis.doc.gov. Russian and independent state business information.

Interstate Statistical Committee of the Commonwealth of Independent States, http://www.cisstat.com

Croatia. Croatian Bureau of Statistics, http://www.dzs.hr

Croatian National Bank, http://www.hnb.hr

Czech Republic. Czech Statistical Office, http://www.czso.cz

Eastern Europe. Central and Eastern Europe Business and Information Center from the U.S. Department of Commerce (CEEBIC), http://www.mac.doc.gov/ceebic

Estonia. Bank of Estonia, http://www.ee/epbe

Greece. National Bank of Greece, http://www.ethniki.gr. Covers Southeastern Europe and the Mediterranean as well as Greece.

National Statistical Service of Greece, http://www.
statistics.gr/ie.htm

Hungary. Hungarian Central Statistical Office,
http://www.ksh.hu/pls/ksh/docs/index.html

Hungarian Ministry of Economic Affairs,
http://www.ikm.iif.hu/english/economy

Magyar Nemzeti Bank (Hungary Central Bank), http://
www.mnb.hu

Kazakhstan. Bank of Kazakhstan, http://www.nationalbank.kz

Kyrgyz Republic. National Statistical Committee of the Kyrgyz
Republic, http://stat-gvc.bishkek.su

Latvia. Latvijas Banka (Central Bank of Latvia), http://www.
bank.lv/latvianindex.html

Lithuania. Department of Statistics to the Government of the
Republic of Lithuania, http://www.std.lt

Lietuvos Bankas (Lithuania), http://www.lbank.lt/home/default.asp

Macedonia. National Bank of the Republic of Macedonia, http://
www.nbrm.gov.mk

State Statistical Office, Republic of Macedonia,
http://www.stat.gov.mk

Moldova. Moldova, MD, http://www.moldova.md

National Bank of Moldova, http://www.bnm.org/index1.html

Poland. National Bank of Poland, http://www.nbp.pl

Polish Market Review Ltd., http://www.polishmarket.com. Polish
economy, emerging economies in Europe.

Polish Official Statistics, http://www.stat.gov.pl

Romania. National Bank of Romania, http://www.bnro.ro

Romania National Institute of Statistics, http://www.insse.ro

Russia. Central Bank of the Russian Federation, http://www.cbr.ru

Slovak Republic. Statistical Office of the Slovak Republic, http://www.statistics.sk

National Bank of Slovakia, http://www.nbs.sk/?INDEXA.htm

Slovenia. SKB Banka D.D., http://www.skb.si. The Slovenian economy.

Statistical Office of the Republic of Slovenia, http://www.sigov.si/zrs

Ukraine. National Bank of Ukraine, http://www.bank.gov.ua

State Committee of Statistics of Ukraine, http://www.ukrstat.gov.ua

Yugoslavia. Federal Republic of Yugoslavia, Federal Statistical Office, http://www.szs.sv.gov.yu

Europe

Civil Society Organisations from the European Commission, http://europa.eu.int/comm/civil_society/coneccs/index_en.htm. European associations and interest groups.

EU Business, http://www.eubusiness.com. Covers all of Europe.

Euro Information, http://www.euro.gov.uk/home.asp?f=1. Official Treasury Euro resource.

European Central Bank, http://www.ecb.int. The euro, balance of payments, interest rates, loans, and other financial statistics.

The European Chemical Industry Home Page, http://www.cefic.be

European Commission, http://europa.eu.int/comm/index_en.htm

European Regions Airlines Association, http://www.eraa.org

The European Union, http://europa.eu.int

Eurostat (Statistical Office of the European Communities), http://europa.eu.int

Forbes European edition, http://www.forbes.com/home_europe

Toy Industries of Europe, http://www.tietoy.org. Covers Europe and the world.

U.N. Economic Commission for Europe, http://www.unece.org/stats/stats_e.htm

Individual European Countries

The listings that follow are composed primarily of national statistical and other government agencies and central banks. Here you will find the following types of information and more:

- Population
- Labor
- Economic indicators
- Environment
- Education
- Energy
- Agriculture
- Transportation
- National accounts
- Investment
- General business

- Currencies

- Trade

- Interest rates

- Banking

- Securities

- Debt

Austria. Austrian Federal Financing Agency, http://www.oebfa. co.at. Economic indicators, budget, debt, bond market, financing instruments.

Austrian Institute of Economic Research, http://www.wifo.ac.at. The Austrian economy.

Austrian National Bank, http://www.oenb.co.at. Financial institutions, interest rates, Austrian capital market, public finances, economic data, international finance.

Statistics Austria, http://www.oestat.gv.at. In German.

Belgium. National Bank of Belgium, http://www.bnb.be/sg/index. htm

Statistics Belgium, http://www.statbel.fgov.be. In English, French, German, and Dutch.

Denmark. Danmark Statistik, http://www.dst.dk/dst/dstframeset_ 1024.asp

Danmarks Nationalbank, http://www.nationalbanken.dk. National Bank of Denmark.

Finland. Bank of Finland, http://www.bof.fi

Statistics Finland, http://www.stat.fi

France. Banque de France, http://www.banque-france.fr

Insee, http://www.insee.fr/fr/home/home_page.asp. France's central statistics agency.

Germany. CESifo Institute for Economic Research, http://www.ifo.de

Deutsche Bundesbank (Central Bank of Germany), http://www.bundesbank.de

Federal Statistical Office Germany, http://www.destatis.de/e_home.htm

Iceland. Central Bank of Iceland, http://www.sedlabanki.is

National Economic Institute Iceland, http://www.ths.is

Statistics Iceland, http://www.statice.is/Welcome.html

Italy. Banca d'Italia, http://www.bancaditalia.it

Statistics Italy, http://www.italyemb.org/Statistics.htm

National Statistical Institute, http://www.istat.it

Luxembourg. Banque Centrale du Luxembourg, http://www.bcl.lu/html/fr/index.html

Statec, http://www.statec.lu

Netherlands. Agricultural Economics Research Institute, http://www.lei.wageningen-ur.nl

De Nederlandsche Bank, http://www.dnb.nl

Netherlands Foreign Trade Agency, http://www.hollandtrade.com. Overall economy and specific industries.

Statistics Netherlands, http://www.cbs.nl

Norway. Norges Bank, http://www.norges-bank.no

Statistics Norway, http://www.ssb.no

Portugal. Banco de Portugal, http://www.bportugal.pt

Instituto Nacional de Estatística Portugal, http://www.ine.pt

Spain. Banco de España, http://www.bde.es

Instituto Nacional de Estadística, http://www.ine.es

Sweden. Riksbank, http://www.riksbank.se

Statistics Sweden, http://www.scb.se

Swedish Trade Council, http://www.swedishtrade.com/cgibin/
start.asp

Switzerland. State Secretariat for Economic Affairs, http://www.
seco-admin.ch/d_index.html

Swiss Federal Statistical Office, http://www.statistik.admin.ch

Swiss National Bank, http://www.snb.ch/d/index3.html

Latin America

Economic Commission for Latin America and the Caribbean,
http://www.eclac.cl

> **When people visit the Fiji Islands, they stay quite a long time: 7.5 days if on business, 8.2 days if on holiday, and 16.9 days if visiting friends and family.**
>
> **Source:** Fiji Islands Statistics Bureau
> **Strategy:** Went to http://www.statsfiji.gov.fj, clicked on Selected Statistics (thinking that tourism would be a major statistic for the country), then Visitors: Average Length of Stay.
> **Cost:** Free.

Argentina. Banco Central de la República Argentina, http://www.bcra.gov.ar

Bolivia. Republica de Bolivia, Instituto Nacional de Estadísticas (INE), http://www.ine.gov.bo

Brazil. Banco Central Do Brasil, http://www.bcb.gov.br/default.asp

Instituto Brasileiro de Geografia e Estatistica, http://www.ibge.gov.br

Chile. Banco Central de Chile, http://www.bcentral.cl

Instituto Nacional de Estadísticas (INE), http://www.ine.cl

Colombia. Departamento Administrativo Nacional de Estadística (DANE), http://www.dane.gov.co. In Spanish.

Mexico. Banco de México, http://www.banxico.org.mx

Instituto Nacional de Estadística Geografía e Informática, http://www.inegi.gob.mx. Environment, economy, population and demographics, society, science and technology. Some in English.

Uruguay. Instituto Nacional de Estadistic (INE), http://www.ine.
gub.uy

Middle East

Arab Ministries from Middle East International Services,
http://www.dalilusa.com/resource_center/arab_ministries.asp (links
to various government agencies such as finance and statistics)

Arabji.com Pan Arab Directory, http://www.arabji.com/index.htm.
Excellent portal to Arab information of all kinds. Highly
recommended.

Countries and Regions from the World Bank, http://web.
worldbank.org/WBSITE/EXTERNAL/COUNTRIES/0,,pagePK:
180619~theSitePK:136917,00.html

Economist Intelligence Unit, EIU Store (use the "Buy Articles"
link), http://www.store.eiu.com. Highly recommended. Reasonable
prices. $

Bahrain. Middle East Directory, Bahrain, http://www.
middleeastdirectory.com/cs_bahrain.htm

Bahrain Monetary Agency, http://www.bma.gov.bh

U.S. Commercial Service, Bahrain, http://www.usatrade.gov/
website/CCG.nsf/ShowCCG?OpenForm&Country=BAHRAIN

Cyprus. Middle East Directory, Cyprus, http://www.
middleeastdirectory.com/cs_cyprus.htm

U.S. Commercial Service, Cyprus, http://www.usatrade.gov/
website/CCG.nsf/ShowCCG?OpenForm&Country=CYPRUS

Djibouti. U.S. Commercial Service, Djibouti, http://www.usatrade.gov/website/CCG.nsf/ShowCCG?OpenForm& Country=DJIBOUTI

Egypt. Middle East Directory, Egypt, http://www. middleeastdirectory.com/cs_egypt.htm

U.S. Commercial Service, Egypt, http://www.usatrade.gov/ website/CCG.nsf/ShowCCG?OpenForm&Country=EGYPT

Iran. Middle East Directory, Iran, http://www.middleeastdirectory.com/cs_iran.htm

Statistical Centre of Iran, http://www.sci.or.ir/

Iraq. Arabji.com, http://www.arabji.com/Iraq/biz.htm

Middle East Directory, Iraq, http://www.middleeastdirectory.com/cs_iraq.htm

U.S. Trade by Commodity with Iraq from the U.S. International Trade Administration, http://www.ita.doc.gov/td/industry/otea/ usfth/top80cty/iraq.html

Israel. Bank of Israel, http://www.bankisrael.gov.il/firsteng.htm

Globes Online, Israel's Business Arena, http://www.globes.co.il/serveen

Israel Central Bureau of Statistics, http://www.cbs.gov.il/engindex.htm

Israel Economic Statistics from GeoInvestor.com, http://www. geoinvestor.com/statistics/israel/economicdata.htm

Israel Ministry of Foreign Affairs, http://www.israel.org/mfa/go.asp?MFAH00040

Jerusalem Post, http://www.jpost.com. $

Jordan. Department of Statistics, Jordan, http://www.dos.gov.jo

Embassy of the Hashemite Kingdom of Jordan, http://www.jordanembassyus.org/new/index.shtml

Middle East Directory, Jordan, http://www.middleeastdirectory.com/cs_jordan.htm

U.S. Commercial Service, Jordan, http://www.usatrade.gov/website/CCG.nsf/ShowCCG?OpenForm&Country=JORDAN

Kuwait. Middle East Directory, Kuwait, http://www.middleeastdirectory.com/cs_kuwait.htm

U.S. Commercial Service, Kuwait, http://www.usatrade.gov/website/CCG.nsf/ShowCCG?OpenForm&Country=KUWAIT

Lebanon. Middle East Directory, Lebanon, http://www.middleeastdirectory.com/cs_lebanon.htm

U.S. Commercial Service, Lebanon, http://www.usatrade.gov/website/CCG.nsf/ShowCCG?OpenForm&Country=LEBANON

Oman. Middle East Directory, Oman, http://www.middleeastdirectory.com/cs_oman.htm

Palestine. Middle East Directory, Palestine, http://www.middleeastdirectory.com/cs_palestine.htm

Qatar. Middle East Directory, Qatar, http://www.middleeastdirectory.com/cs_qatar.htm

U.S. Commercial Service, Qatar, http://www.usatrade.gov/website/CCG.nsf/ShowCCG?OpenForm&Country=QATAR

Saudi Arabia. Middle East Directory, Saudi Arabia, http://www.middleeastdirectory.com/cs_saudi.htm

Saudi Arabian Embassy in the U.S., http://www.saudiembassy.net (See the newsroom.)

U.S. Commercial Service, Saudi Arabia, http://www.usatrade.gov/ website/CCG.nsf/ShowCCG?OpenForm&Country=SAUDI+ ARABIA

Syria. Middle East Directory, Syria, http://www. middleeastdirectory.com/cs_syria.htm

U.S. Commercial Service, Syria, http://www.usatrade.gov/website/ CCG.nsf/ShowCCG?OpenForm&Country=SYRIA

Turkey. Middle East Directory, Turkey, http://www. middleeastdirectory.com/cs_turkey.htm

Turkish Economy from GeoInvestor.com, http://www.geoinvestor.com/countries/turkey/main.htm

U.S. Commercial Service, Turkey, http://www.usatrade.gov/ website/CCG.nsf/ShowCCG?OpenForm&Country=TURKEY

Central Bank of the Republic of Turkey, http://www.tcmb.gov.tr

Republic of Turkey, State Institute of Statistics, http://www. die.gov.tr.

United Arab Emirates. Middle East Directory, United Arab Emirates, http://www.middleeastdirectory.com/cs_uae.htm

U.S. Commercial Service, United Arab Emirates, http:// www.usatrade.gov/website/CCG.nsf/ShowCCG?OpenForm& Country=UAE

Yemen. Middle East Directory, Yemen, http://www. middleeastdirectory.com/cs_yemen.htm

U.S. Commercial Service, Yemen, http://www.usatrade.gov/ website/CCG.nsf/ShowCCG?OpenForm&Country=YEMEN

West Bank and Gaza. U.S. Commercial Service, West Bank and Gaza, http://www.usatrade.gov/website/CCG.nsf/ShowCCG? OpenForm&Country=WEST+BANK

World
General

CIA World Factbook, http://www.odci.gov/cia/publications/ factbook/index.html. Basic information about countries.

Data Intal, http://estadisticas.sieca.org.gt/dataintalweb. Imports and exports in the Americas.

Foreign Trade Statistics from the U.S. Census Bureau, http://www. census.gov/foreign-trade/www

International Labour Organization Bureau of Statistics, http://www. ilo.org/public/english/bureau/stat/intro

Market Research and Industry Sector Analysis Reports for countries around the world from the U.S. Department of Commerce, http://www.tradeport.org/ts/countries

NewsBase World Monitoring, http://www.newsbaseworldmonitoring. com. Monitors business and political news reports from 150 countries. Each article costs a few cents. You accrue charges up to a certain amount before you have to pay. You can see articles without having paid for them, but if you don't pay, you will be cut off from access to the site. $

OECD (Organisation for Economic Co-operation and Development) http://www.oecd.org/EN/home/0,,EN-home-0-nodirectorate-no-no-no-0,FF.html. Covers every aspect of its 30 member countries, including Europe, Canada, Australia, Japan, Korea, Mexico, New Zealand, Turkey, the U.K., and the U.S.

Official Statistics on the Web, http://www.auckland.ac.nz/lbr/stats/offstats/OFFSTATSmain.htm. Metasite that provides links to statistical sites from official sources around the world. By country, region, and topic.

The Paperboy, http://www.thepaperboy.com.au/welcome.html. Identify and go straight to newspapers around the world; search headlines of major news sources through one interface. Ridiculously inexpensive. $ There are world, U.K., and Canadian editions.

SI Trends, http://www.sitrends.org/statistics. Trends in service industries around the world.

Statistical Data Locators from Nanyang Technological University Library, http://www.ntu.edu.sg/library/stat/statdata.htm. International trade and socioeconomic data for countries around the world.

UNICEF, http://www.unicef.org/statis. The world's children.

United Nations Industrial Development Organization, http://www.unido.org. Industrial statistics from selected countries.

United Nations InfoNation, http://www.cyberschoolbus.un.org/infonation/info.asp. Country indicators.

United Nations Statistics Division, http://unstats.un.org/unsd. Industry, housing, environment, energy, society, national accounts, trade.

U.S. Commercial Service, http://www.usatrade.gov. Market and industry research for U.S. exporters. Covers the world.

World Chambers Network, http://www.worldchambers.com. Chambers of commerce around the world. Great for local business and industry information as well as demographics.

World Economic Forum, http://www.weforum.org. Global competitiveness report. Free country reports covering various issues like technology, health, and agriculture. $

The World Gazetteer, http://www.gazetteer.de. Population figures for cities, towns, and places of countries around the world.

Agriculture, Environment, and Natural Resources

Food and Agriculture Organization of the United Nations, http://www.fao.org

Energy, Minerals, and Metals

British Petroleum Statistical Review of World Energy, http://www.bp.com/index.asp

International Iron and Steel Institute, http://www.worldsteel.org

Financial Services

Bank for International Settlements, http://www.bis.org. International banking statistics.

Central Bank Web sites from Bank for International Settlements, http://www.bis.org/cbanks1.htm

International Monetary Fund (IMF), http://www.imf.org

World Bank Data and Statistics, http://www.worldbank.org/data. Global development statistics.

World Investment Report (United Nations Conference on Trade and Development), http://www.unctad.org/wir/index.htm. Foreign direct investment by the world's nations.

Information Technology and Communications

Ebusiness Forum from The Economist Business Intelligence Unit, http://www.ebusinessforum.com

Global Reach, http://www.glreach.com/globstats/index.php3. Numbers of people online in various languages.

International Telecommunication Union, http://www.itu.int/home/index.html

Internet Domain Survey from the Internet Software Consortium, http://www.isc.org/ds

ZDNet, http://www.zdnet.com. Computing around the world.

Media, Publishing, Printing, and Broadcasting

International Publishers Association, http://www.ipa-uie.org

Transportation

International Air Transport Association, http://www.iata.org

Travel and Tourism

World Tourism Organization, http://www.world-tourism.org

Chapter 7

Market Research Sources

Market research tends to be very expensive. If you can't find what you want using the other methods in this book, you may have to spring for a report that costs upward of a couple thousand dollars. However, there are some things you can try first. Tip: Before you buy an expensive report, check for press releases on the Web site of the company that produced it. You may find everything you need right there.

Metasites

All of the following metasites are free to search. However, most of the resources they lead to cost money.

Corporate Information, http://www.corporateinformation.com. International. $

Valuation Resources Industry Resources Reports, http://www. valuationresources.com/IndustryReport.htm. Metasite leading to a variety of impressive resources from trade associations, industry publications, and research firms. $

Mindbranch, http://www.mindbranch.com. Coverage of many industries and countries. $

Market Research on the Web from IRN Services, http://www. irn-research.com. Market research metasite. $

Buy by the Page or Section

Some services let you browse tables of contents and lists of figures/tables, then buy portions of market research reports. They include the following:

DialogSelect, http://www.dialog.com. Provides a pay-as-you-go service. $

Marketresearch.com, http://www.marketresearch.com. Offers a service they call "Buy by the slice." Reports come from more than 350 publishers. Prices vary. $

Freedonia, http://freedoniagroup.com. $30 per record (page). $

ECNext, http://www.ecnext.com. Some reports are available in sections. You can also search ECNext's collection of statistical tables! $

Reasonably Priced Reports

BizAdvantage, http://www.bizadvantage.com. Datamonitor industry reports for $100. $

BizMiner, http://www.bizminer.com/market_research.asp. U.S. only. $

BizProLink, http://www.bizprolink.com, provides portals to 43 industries. Each portal has a link and search facility leading to market research reports. $

California Retail Survey, http://californiaretailsurvey.netfirms.com. In-depth information on 500 California retail markets. Some information is free, but the bulk is contained in one priced publication.

First Research, http://www.1stresearch.com. Industry overviews. $

Harris InfoSource, http://www.harrisinfo.com. Offers 95 industry reports. $

IBIS World, http://www.ibisworld.com. Slightly above reasonable prices but worth mentioning. All reports $425 each. $

JT Research LLC, http://industryresearch.com. Off-the-shelf reports start at $100. $

U.S. Business Reporter, http://www.activemedia-guide.com/prospectus_cp.htm. Free industry overviews.

Research@Economy.com, http://www.economy.com/research/default. asp. Each four-page report is $200. A one-year subscription (basic report plus three updates) runs $500. $

Other

IRS Market Segmentation Specialization Program, http://www.irs. gov. Fascinating guidelines for tax auditors specializing in various industries. Insight into and some statistics on the industries provided.

Just-Drinks, http://www.just-drinks.com. Market research on segments of the beverage industry around the world. Not cheap, but included here because of the quality and focus of the site. Some articles are free. $

Report Finder from Midnight Croquet, http://www.the-list.co.uk. U.K. market research reports. $

U.S. Commercial Service, http://www.usatrade.gov. Market and industry research for U.S. exporters. Covers the world.

Market Research Companies

You can often find free information in press releases and other areas of market research company Web sites. Most companies specialize in one or several related areas, though some generalize. Some can be very snooty, restricting even the most basic information to their "clients" only. (As you can tell, this is a philosophy I find highly repugnant.) Here's a list of some of the best, including some of the snooty ones:

Datamonitor, http://www.datamonitor.com. International business and the consumer markets. $

Economist Intelligence Unit, http://www.eiu.com. Automotive industry, healthcare, telecommunications, country reports. $

Euromonitor, http://www.euromonitor.com. Consumer goods and services around the world. $

IDC, http://www.idc.com. Information technology. $

Forrester Research, http://www.forrester.com. Information technology. $

Frost & Sullivan, http://www.frost.com. Technology. $

Financial Times, http://www.ft.com. Wide range of coverage. $

Freedonia Group, http://www.freedonia.com. A variety of industries. $

Gartner Group, http://www.gartner.com. Information technology. $

IMS Global Health Services, http://www.ims-global.com. $

Key Note, http://www.keynote.co.uk. U.K. market research. $

MBD (Market & Business Development), http://www. marketresearchonthe.net/site/frameset.asp. U.K. market research. $

Mintel, http://www.reports.mintel.com. Consumer goods and services. $

MTI, http://www.marketfile.com. U.K. and worldwide market research. $

Mori, http://www.mori.com. U.K. market and public opinion research. Some free. $

Reuters Business Insight, http://www.reutersbusinessinsight.com. Various industries. $

SMI-Online, http://www.smi-online.co.uk. Global and European market research. $

Snapshots International, http://www.snapdata.com. Market overviews for various countries and industries.

Chapter 8

Economic and Financial Statistics

How Economic Data Are Gathered

Economic indicators are based on national income and product account figures; monthly surveys focusing on employment/unemployment and prices of consumer goods; surveys of purchasing agents and their views on inventories, orders, and prices; and similar data. Some of this data is "adjusted" to compensate for seasonal variations before the indicator is calculated. Indicators are supposed to be representative of an economy as a whole, and may be of three types: leading, coincident, or lagging. *Leading* indicators predict a turning point, *coincident* indicators indicate the current state of affairs, and *lagging* indicators show up after a trend is already occurring and verify that it is, in fact, doing so.

The U.S. Consumer Price Index (CPI) and similar indicators are calculated from survey data by the Bureau of Labor Statistics and other agencies. Did you know that the Consumer Price Index measures goods and services purchased by *wage earners and clerical workers only*? It is *not* a general cost of living index. Surprise!

Prices, interest rates, yields, and trading volumes derive from stock and commodity exchange bulletins, documents, and lists, as well as banks and other financial institutions.

Other sources of financial and economic data include:

- Bank and analyst reports
- Banks and mortgage bankers

- Credit institutions
- Insurance companies
- Interviews (phone, mail, in-person)
- Municipalities and states (property taxes and real estate statistics)
- Mutual fund managers
- Newspapers, wires, journals
- U.S. Bureau of the Census

The sources in this chapter will lead you to the following types of information:

Banking and Currency

- ATM and other computer use in banking
- Bank, credit union, savings and loan assets, liabilities, deposits
- Banker salaries and demographics
- Credit
- Currencies
- Electronic funds transfers
- Loans
- Precious metals

Economic Indicators

- Consumer price index
- Consumer spending
- Discount rate
- Employment and unemployment
- Gross national and domestic products
- Inflation
- Interest rates and yields
- Prime lending rate
- Producer price index

- Stock market indices

Insurance
- Claims
- Demographics of claimants, insureds
- Insurance agent earnings and demographics
- Premiums

Investment
- Dividends
- Earnings per share, price/earnings ratios
- Investment rate
- Management fees
- Mutual funds
- Securities and investment vehicle prices
- Stock broker earnings, demographics
- Stock market indexes
- Technical stock market measures

Real Estate
- Loan interest rates
- Property taxes
- Real estate agents and brokers
- Real estate trusts
- Real estate values, sales

Personal Finance
- Family expenditures; ratio of house and other payments to total income
- Savings rate

Trade

- Exports

- Imports

United States
General

Administrative Office of the U.S. Courts, http://www.uscourts.gov/
Press_Releases/index.html. Bankruptcies.

The Beige Book, http://www.federalreserve.gov/fomc/beigebook/
2002. Current economic conditions.

Economic Policy Institute, http://epinet.org. Living standards, labor
markets, government, the economy, trade, globalization, education,
sustainable economics.

Economic Statistics Briefing Room, http://www.whitehouse.gov/
fsbr/esbr.html. Employment, income, money, production, prices,
transportation, output, international.

EconSearch, http://www.inomics.com/cgi/show. Portal and search
engine for economists. Powerful, but requires patience.

Federal Reserve Bank of Cleveland, http://www.clevelandfed.org/
index.cfm Consumer price index, interest rates, money and financial
markets, economic activity, labor markets, inflation, Federal Deposit
Insurance Corporation funds, foreign central banks.

Federal Reserve Statistical Releases, http://www.federalreserve.gov/
releases. Foreign exchange rates, interest rates, money supply, consumer credit, industrial production, flow of funds.

Infoplease.com, http://infoplease.com. Labor, poverty and income, U.S. economy, Federal budget, social security, direct foreign investment, new businesses, business failures, corporate profits, stock market.

Internal Revenue Service Tax Stats, http://www.irs.gov. Individuals, businesses, charities and nonprofits, government, retirement plans, tax professionals. Totals and by general industry.

National Bureau of Economic Research, http://www.nber.org. General economic data, business cycle dates, and a variety of economic analysis working papers available for a small fee. Most of the site is free. $

Panel Study of Income Dynamics from the University of Michigan's Institute for Social Research, http://www.umich.edu/~psid/index.html

Statistical Abstract of the United States, http://www.census.gov/ statab/www. Published annually. Federal budget is in Federal Government Finances and Employment section.

U.S. Business Advisor, http://www.business.gov. Government statistics from a variety of agencies covering labor, social security, family, transportation, agriculture, wildlife, education, environment, health, energy, banking, crime, demographics, and the economy.

U.S. Census Bureau, County Business Patterns, http://www.census. gov/epcd/cbp/view/cbpview.html. Economic profiles at the local level.

U.S. Census Bureau Economic Census, http://www.census.gov/ econ/www/econ_cen.html. Conducted every five years.

U.S. Department of Commerce Bureau of Economic Analysis, http://www.bea.doc.gov. National, industry, international, and regional data. Includes Survey of Current Business.

U.S. Industry and Trade Outlook, http://www.ita.doc.gov/td/ industry/otea/outlook/index.html. This classic source was not available on the Web at press time, but many of the data are available elsewhere on government Web sites. You can also order a CD-ROM or print version.

Cost of Living

ACCRA Cost of Living Index, http://www.coli.org. Compares cost of living for North American cities. Reasonable prices. $

AIER Cost-of-Living Calculator, http://www.aier.org/colcalc.html. Converts dollars from any one year to any other year.

Average Price Data from the Bureau of Labor Statistics, http://146.142.4.24/cgi-bin/surveymost?ap. Current and historical prices for selected commodities, including energy.

Cost of Living Index, http://nt.mortgage101.com/partner-scripts/ 1150.asp?p=atmtg. Cost of living for 100 U.S. cities.

The Inflation Calculator, http://www.westegg.com/inflation. Adjust for inflation for any year between 1800 and the present.

Inflation Conversion Factors for Dollars 1665 to Estimated 2012, Robert Sahr at Oregon State University, http://www.orst.edu/dept/ pol_sci/fac/sahr/sahr.htm

Martindale's "The Reference Desk," http://www-sci.lib.uci.edu/ HSG/RefCalculators.html. Metasite containing links to more than 15,000 calculators covering business, economics, personal finance, energy, and more. Superb!

NewsEngin Cost of Living Calculator, http://www.newsengin.com/ neFreeTools.nsf/CPIcalc. Compares cost of living for cities and regions of the U.S. for various years.

Finance

Census of Finance, Insurance, and Real Estate, U.S. Bureau of the Census, http://www.census.gov/svsd/www/economic.html. Published every five years.

CNNMoney, http://money.cnn.com. All aspects of money.

Financial Data Finder (Department of Finance Ohio State University), http://fisher.osu.edu/fin/osudata.htm

Quicken Financial Network, http://www.quicken.com. Mutual funds, free and low cost analyst research reports, company financial comparisons, etc.

Government

Consolidated Federal Funds Report, Federal, State, and Local Governments, http://www.census.gov/ftp/pub/govs/www/cffr.html. Federal expenditures or obligations for grants, salaries, wages, procurement contracts, direct payments, loans, and insurance for the states, District of Columbia, and U.S. territories.

The Green Book Overview of Entitlement Programs, http://aspe.hhs. gov. Social security and Medicare. See http://aspe.hhs.gov/2000gb/ index.htm for the 2000 *Green Book*.

Social Security Administration Office of Policy, http://www.ssa.gov/ policy. Profiles of social security recipients; earnings and employment of workers eligible for social security.

U.S. Department of Defense Procurement Statistics (Procurement and Economic Information Division), http://web1.whs.osd.mil/ peidhome/peidhome.htm

Healthcare

Centers for Medicare & Medicaid Services, http://cms.hhs.gov. Healthcare expenditures and prices.

Health insurance data from the U.S. Census Bureau, http://www.census.gov/ftp/pub/hhes/www/hlthins.html

Labor

Abbott, Langer & Associates Compensation and Benefits Reports, http://www.abbott-langer.com

Bureau of Labor Statistics, http://stats.bls.gov. Consumer Price Index, wages, income, employment and unemployment, productivity, employee benefits, labor costs, consumer expenditures, injuries and illnesses, demographics of the labor force, collective bargaining, and more.

Science and Engineering Indicators from the National Science Foundation, http://www.nsf.gov/nsb. Patents, employment for scientists and engineers.

Real Estate

CoStar Group, http://www.costar.com. U.S. real estate. Building-specific information on 800,000 properties, including comparable sales, cap rates, income and expense data, lease expirations and loan terms. Covers "virtually every building in every major city" and six million tenants, owners, and brokers. General market trends are free. $

Grubb & Ellis, http://www.grubb-ellis.com. U.S. Market Trends is Grubb & Ellis' quarterly report on national market conditions, including the office, industrial, retail, multihousing, and telecom markets.

Realtor.com, http://www.realtor.com. U.S. home prices.

Realtor.org, http://www.realtor.org. U.S. home prices by metro area and state, apartment/condo/co-op prices by state, housing affordability index, etc.

Regional and Local Economies

County and City Data Book, U.S. Bureau of the Census, http://www.census.gov/statab/www/ccdb.html

Research@Economy.com, http://www.economy.com/research/default. asp. Profiles of local areas, states, countries, industries. Includes cost of living, forecasts, real estate, and patent profiles. $

Salaries

Computerjobs.com, http://www.computerjobs.com/homepage.aspx. U.S. only.

Homefair.com Salary Calculator, http://www.homefair.com/ homefair/calc/salcalc.html

JobStar, http://jobstar.org/index.cfm. Sponsored by libraries in the state of California, this excellent site links to more than 300 salary surveys on the Web. Also links to cost of living surveys for the U.S. in general and California specifically.

Salary.com cost-of-living wizard, http://www.salary.com

Salaryexpert.com, http://www.salaryexpert.com. Cost of living, salaries, employee benefits. Much is free. Reports are reasonably priced. $

Australia and New Zealand

See also Chapter 6.

Cost of living calculator for Australia, http://www.ex.ac.uk/cimt/res2/calcs/calcolau.htm. 1930 to 2009.

National Remuneration Centre (Australia), http://www.natrem.com. au. Pay rates and links to salary surveys. $

SalaryZone, http://www.salaryzone.com.au. Salaries in Australia. Information technology, banking, finance, accounting, and office support.

Wage$.com.au, http://www.wages.com.au. Wages in Australia. Also links to other salary sites around the world.

Canada

See also Chapter 6.

Bank of Canada, http://www.banqueducanada.ca

Canadian Labour Market Information, http://lmi-imt.hrdc-drhc.gc.ca. Salaries and employment levels.

e-Space Connections, http://www.e-space.com. Canadian commercial real estate.

Royal LePage, http://www.royallepage.com. Canadian office and commercial property.

Ireland

See also Chapter 6.

Executive Salaries in Ireland, http://www.ireland.com/jobs/advice/ salary.htm

Finfacts, http://www.finfacts.com. Irish finance portal. Everything from milk statistics to salary surveys to the Irish markets.

Jobs in Ireland, http://www.topjobs.ie. Irish salaries.

United Kingdom and Northern Ireland

See also Chapter 6.

Regional U.K. Salary Calculator, http://www.reed.co.uk/cgi-bin/ calculator.asp

SalarySearch, http://www.salarysearch.co.uk. U.K. salaries and benefits. $

World

See also Chapter 6.

In addition to these sources, search Factiva for office space prices and vacancy rates around the world.

CB Richard Ellis, http://www.cbrichardellis.com. Office rents, vacancy rates, and occupancy costs worldwide.

Center for Defense Information, http://www.cdi.org. Arms trade database, military spending.

Collier's International Market Reports, http://www.colliers.com/fr_ market.html. Real estate around the world. Some is a bit old, but much is quite usable.

Consumer Research Center, http://www.conference-board.org/ products/c-consumer.cfm. Consumer confidence, help-wanted index, business confidence, leading indexes for select countries.

Cushman & Wakefield, http://www.cushmanwakefield.com/ globhome.html. Real estate market summaries around the world.

Economic Cycle Research Institute, http://www.businesscycle.com. Indicators for countries, regions, and industries.

The Economist, http://www.economist.com. Business worldwide. Reasonable prices, or free to subscribers. $

Euromoney.com, http://www.euromoney.com. Money and capital markets around the world.

Infonation, http://www.cyberschoolbus.un.org/infonation/index.asp. Country economic indicators at a glance.

Institute for Markets in Transition of the Helsinki School of Economics and Business Administration, http://www.balticdata.info. For the Baltics.

Inter-American Development Bank, http://www.iadb.org. Economic information about the Americas.

International cost of living calculator, http://www1.moneymanager. com.au/mm2/personal_finance/calcs/costliving.html

International Monetary Fund, http://www.imf.org/external

International Trade Administration, U.S. Department of Commerce, http://www.ita.doc.gov. Trade data sliced a variety of ways, including by industry and country.

The Journal of Commerce, http://www.joc.com. International trade, banking and finance, insurance, maritime industries.

Oanda.com Currencies Converter, http://www.oanda.com/cgi-bin/ncc. Converts 164 currencies and precious metals.

Office of Management and Budget: Budget Publications and Economic Report of the President, http://www.gpo.gov/usbudget/index.html. Includes historical expenditures back to the 1920s.

Oncor International, http://www.oncorintl.com/Default.asp?bhcp=1. European and North American office property reports plus South Africa, Mexico, and Brazil.

Organisation for Economic Cooperation and Development (OECD) Statistics Directorate, http://www.oecd.org. International trade, agriculture, industry and services, national accounts, finance, leading indicators and tendencies, prices, purchasing power, statistics for nonmember countries. There are 30 member countries.

Organization of American States Trade Unit, http://www.sice.oas.org

United Nations Statistics Division, http://unstats.un.org/unsd

World Bank, http://www.worldbank.org

World Trade Organization, http://www.wto.org

The number of bad debts for bank and financial intermediary loans in Italy rose from 76,775 in September 2001 to 78,019 in December 2001

Source: Central Bank of Italy

Strategy: Went to http://www.bancaditalia.it and clicked on "English." Selected Statistics, then Statistical Bulletin. Selected the most recent in PDF format, then Information on Customers.

Cost: Free.

Extended Case Study: How the September 11th, 2001 Terrorist Attacks Have Affected the U.S. Economy.

Purpose: This case study demonstrates how to find the impact of a major event on the U.S. economy. It points out the difficulty of getting current information packaged exactly the way you want it, despite the notoriety and overwhelming economic impact of the triggering event.

Sources: Factiva, Google, Bureau of Economic Analysis

This question should have been amply covered in the media, so we could search for newspaper and journal articles to answer it. There will also be specific information from the Insurance Information Institute having to do with insurance costs, perhaps from the Travel Industry Association about the effect on tourism, as well as from airline industry analysts, the Bureau of Transportation Statistics, and so on.

To find general articles, I started with Factiva. I looked for *terrorism and impact w/2 economy* in the headline and lead paragraph for the current year in major news and business publications. This strategy was quite broad, not specifically referring to September 11th in any way, and yet I felt that it might be a good one because the terms "terrorism" and "September 11" have virtually become synonymous.

I found an article that began "The lack of available terrorism insurance for U.S. businesses is beginning to impact the broader economy with a cost equal to 1 percent of the gross domestic product, U.S. Treasury Secretary Paul O'Neill...." The article was published by *Dow Jones International News* on April 30, 2002, well after the attacks. The time lapse was a good sign. It takes a while to feel and assess economic impacts from catastrophic events.

That was not a bad answer, but I wanted to look for something more recent and general, not just something relating to terrorism insurance. I tried another strategy:

September 11 and impact w/2 economy in the full text of the article

This approach yielded an article that confirmed the Treasury Secretary's estimate. Here is a quote from "Terror Insurance Pervasive, Drag on U.S. Economy" from *Dow Jones Capital Markets Report* from February 2002. It began "The lack of affordable coverage in the post-Sept. 11 insurance market will unduly burden the U.S. economy's...." My problem with this article was that it was written fairly close to September 11, which meant that it couldn't possibly include the total assessment, which may not have been available until significantly later, and that it too addressed the subject of terrorism insurance. I wanted to know how much money has been lost through not only damage but also reduced spending.

I decided to step back a moment and conduct a general Web search just to see what might turn up. Here is my Google strategy:

September 11 impact economy

This strategy yielded better results. The first good hit was an article on the Ernst & Young Web site at http://www.ey.com/ GLOBAL/content.nsf/International/Article_-_Assessing_the_ Impact_of_September_11 called "Assessing the Impact of September 11." While the article was written in 2001, hence lacking perspective, it did offer a number of useful facts:

The proximate cause of this projected contraction was the gigantic losses from the attacks: $13 billion of destroyed private and government equity, an estimated $35 billion to $50 billion of insured losses, and extreme stock market volatility that wiped out $1.2 trillion of equity portfolio values in the first week after trading resumed, only to restore it weeks later.

The immediate effect of the disaster was to accelerate the contraction of the U.S. economy, already languishing in the months before the attacks. Soon after the event, forecasters projected a slowdown in GDP of 1.4% or more in the third quarter of 2001, slashing growth to minus 0.9% and moving the economy officially into recession territory. Early third quarter measures suggest a slightly better environment, with the economy contracting at a 0.4% rate. Initial fourth-quarter estimates were for a steep contraction of 3%, but currently the slowdown looks slightly weaker, perhaps in the 1.3% to 1.5% range.

The article went on to analyze the effect on certain types of spending, such as software and equipment, construction, trade, and oil prices. The article was helpful in that it provided measures of overall impact to the GDP, but they were so close to the event that they didn't tell the whole story. Again, the date was a problem.

One reality this search points out is the difficulty of finding numbers packaged exactly as you want them. I was getting the type of answers I wanted, but they were too old. The articles that were recent enough seemed to deal only with segments of the economy rather than the whole picture. I tried another strategy, again on Google.

September 11 "overall impact" economy

Even this strategy yielded segmented results, such as the fact that the overall impact of September 11 on the restaurant business exceeded $1 billion in September alone.

If I kept pursuing this approach, I might have found the answer. However, I wanted to try another strategy. I often switch strategies completely in the middle of a search just to see how my ideas will pan out. If they don't work, I may revisit those I have already tried, looking farther down the list of hits.

Here was my new idea. Government agencies and think tanks need to assess the impact of September 11. They may have produced something useful. One possibility was the Bureau of Economic Analysis (BEA), which is part of the Department of Commerce. Its site is http://www.bea.doc.gov.

I found a useful article there, though it too was from 2001. I selected the link for BEA's economic accounts, National, Articles. There, under the heading for Disasters, I found "The Terrorist Attacks of September 11th as Reflected in the National Income and Product Accounts" from November 2001. National accounts is government finance, not the economy as a whole, but I started reading the article anyway. Within it I found a curious but relevant statement: "Because most of the effects are embedded in the source data and cannot be separately identified, BEA did not attempt to quantify the total impact of the attacks on gross domestic product (GDP) or on other major aggregates." Did this mean I wouldn't be able to find the answer at all? I found that hard to believe.

When I looked a little further, I saw that the BEA had included a table at the end of the document that gave a sort-of answer to my question, at least as of November 2001. The table was titled "Adjustments to the NIPA's for the Impact of the September 11th Terrorist Attacks, 2001: III," and it showed the reduction in billions of dollars to each line item on both product and income sides. Personal consumption expenditures were down $21 billion; wages and salaries $2.5 billion; and corporate profits $39 billion. Some other items went up: net exports $44 billion and consumption of fixed capital by private enterprise $62 billion. This information was helpful, but again, it didn't completely answer my question.

When I start dancing around the answer as I am here, I step back and think about whether I am indeed asking the right question. Sometimes I am not. There are usually multiple ways to frame a question to get a usable answer. Is it possible that there is no way to assess the overall economic impact of September 11th on the U.S.? How else can I express what I want? Am I destined to find the effect only on New York City, or the airline industry, or the insurance industry? Is the topic so broad that the information about it is enough to drown me? Is it too soon to get the answer to this question?

While it is true that there is and will continue to be massive amounts of information about my topic, the last question may be the key to my problem. Remembering that statistics take some time to gather and analyze, I realized that it might be quite some time until we know the complete economic impact. (Those of you who have read *Finding Statistics Online* may remember that I had the same problem in the case study that attempted to assess the economic impact of the 1994 Northridge earthquake.) I may have been premature, which was no reason not to ask the question. Being so only meant that I might get incomplete answers for a while.

Before I left this search, I wanted to try one more thing: very focused phrase searching as described in Chapter 4. I hadn't actually done that yet. All my strategies so far involved keywords.

When I tried *"economic impact of September 11th,"* I got a variety of hits having to do with the impact on this or that geographical area or particular sector of the economy. There was nothing wrong with my strategy. The problem was the overwhelming number of articles, many of which were too narrowly focused for my purposes. When I tried *"overall economic impact of September 11th,"* I got no hits at all. Nor did *"economic impact of September 11th on the U.S. economy"* get me anything useful. Because I was sure there was an answer out there, the way to proceed was to continue tweaking my terminology, perhaps combining phrases with keywords, as in something like *"economic impact of 9/11" U.S. economy 2002* (the 2002 was to see if I could limit the search to articles published in 2002, the current year as I write this case study) and trying other sources. This is one of those searches that necessitates a lot of detail work and patience. You just have to keep plodding through it.

Lessons Learned

✔ Sometimes the easiest-looking questions are the most difficult to answer. One reason may be that there are so many facets to the topic that it is hard to zoom in on the big picture.

✔ You may need to try a wide variety of strategies, both in wording and in sources.

✔ Finding recent information can be tricky. Sometimes including the current year in your keywords helps.

✔ Make sure you are asking the right question.

Chapter 9

Company Information

How Company Information Is Gathered

Company financial statistics come from interim and annual reports, public filings, regulatory reports, proxy reports, prospectuses, credit reports, and news releases. Remember that for private companies, news reports and press releases can be effective. Public company information is just that: public, which means that it is easily obtained. However, public companies only have to disclose so much about their operations, so you may face challenges in getting detailed information.

The sources listed in this chapter include article aggregators, company directories, government agencies that oversee company registrations and activities, credit report providers, and others.

Types of Data

Types of company information you can find include:

- Balance sheets
- Capacities
- Cash flow
- Earnings information
- Income statements
- Numbers of employees
- Ownership

161

Searching for companies with certain revenues

If you want to search for companies with revenues of a certain amount, either by product or some other parameter like geographical area, you will need to use a powerful system like DIALOG (http://www.dialog.com), the Kompass service (http://www.kompass.com), LexisNexis (http://www.lexisnexis.com), Factiva (http://www.factiva.com), or Hoover's (http://www.hoovers.com). The ability to search by revenue is a value-added service that, unfortunately, will cost you.

If you conduct such searches, beware. Make sure that the database(s) you are using cover the companies you're interested in. Check the criteria for inclusion and the scope. Many databases do not cover private companies, for example, and it may be difficult to tell that. If the companies are not selected systematically, there could be gaps in coverage, which you will have to remedy by searching multiple databases. If you are not an experienced searcher on the particular system, call customer service and get them to give you a search strategy, or hire a professional to do the search for you (you can find independent researchers through the Association of Independent Information Professionals, AIIP, at http://www.aiip.org).

If you are looking only for a small number of companies, as long as you have already identified them you can skip the expensive database search and look up each company individually. If the companies are public, you will be able to find their revenues easily by looking at their 10-Ks, the annual financial statements they must file with the Securities and Exchange Commission, or public filings of non-U.S. companies available through their respective regulatory agencies.

If you are looking for private U.S. companies in a certain revenue range, you have your work cut out for you. (Not so with U.K. private companies, which must file their financial information with Companies House [http://www.companies-house.gov.uk], where it is available to the public.) Private company financial information is available on a few databases available through DIALOG, LexisNexis, Hoovers, Factiva, and Kompass, but coverage is spotty.

To recap: To search U.S. public companies by revenue or some other parameter is a relatively easy but expensive matter. For private companies, some databases will provide coverage, but there may be holes, and searching them is expensive. You can find some private company financial information via news and press releases, but there is no way to power search according to a particular criterion and be sure that you get complete results.

United States

See also World.

AM Best, http://www.ambest.com. Insurance company ratings.

Bizjournals.com, http://www.bizjournals.com. In addition to searching its archives of many U.S. local papers, you can sign up to be notified by e-mail when a headline mentions your target company.

Bloomberg, http://www.bloomberg.com. U.S. and foreign company news as well as the securities markets. Some information is free. Reasonable prices for articles. $

Business Credit USA, http://www.businesscreditusa.com. Approximate sales volume available (reports give ranges) as well as number of employees for the last three years. Also lists lawsuits and identifies competitors. U.S. and Canadian companies. Very reasonable prices. $

CAROL, http://www.carol.co.uk. European, U.S., and Australian company annual reports.

C/Net, http://www.cnet.com. Computing, communications, media, e-business, personal technology.

Corporate Information, http://www.corporateinformation.com. Companies and industries around the world. While many of the links the searches lead you to are dead, you can identify potential sources. Requires some patience, but can be rewarding. It's free, though it can lead you to pay sites.

DialogSelect, http://www.dialog.com. Provides a pay-as-you-go service. $

FindArticles.com, http://www.FindArticles.com

Forbes 500 Largest Private Companies, http://www.forbes.com/private500

The Inc 500 Fastest-Growing Companies, http://www.inc.com/inc500

NASDAQ, http://www.nasdaq.com. When you enter a company's symbol, you can get recent company news, fundamentals, stock chart, and an analyst brief, and you can identify major competitors and get information about their stocks. You also get links to the company's SEC filings.

NASDAQ News Finder, http://www.nasdaqnews.com. Search for NASDAQ companies by name, partial name, and ticker, and sort by total market value. You can also search by state and/or ZIP code.

LexisNexis, http://www.lexisnexis.com. Use the pay-by-credit-card feature. Reasonable prices. Don't miss the corporate affiliations service. $

Report Gallery, http://www.reportgallery.com/new-look/home.htm. Annual reports from 2,200 companies.

RMA (The Risk Management Association), http://www.rmahq.com/Ann_Studies/asstudies.html. Annual statement studies provide benchmark financial data based on financial statements from small and medium-sized companies. Available by SIC or NAICS code. Balance sheets, income statements, etc. $

The Wall Street Transcript, http://www.twst.com. Some excerpts from CEO and analyst interviews are free. All kinds of financial, unit sales, and market information!

ZDNet, http://www.zdnet.com. Computing industry.

Finding private company financials by searching articles

Dolby Laboratories
"Dolby, privately held since Ray Dolby founded it in 1965, did $133 million in sales during fiscal 2000 and employs about 550."
Source: San Francisco Business Times, December 11, 2001
Strategy: Searched http://www.bizjournals.com using *+dolby +laboratories* in articles for the past year. Came up with an article titled "Dolby Labs plugs $3M into Lake Technology." The last paragraph gives summary financials for fiscal 2000. Another article from the same source tells us that as of May 31, 2002, Dolby had sold more than 1 billion licensed products containing its sound technologies.
Cost: Free.

Finding information on a private company by looking at its Web site

Dolby Labs and Hallmark Cards, Inc.
The Dolby Laboratories Web site (http://www.dolby.com) provides a wealth of information about Dolby's business models and the number of licenses the company has sold. (Dolby noise reduction technology is the gold standard for audio around the world. The company licenses its technology for use in a variety of products, such as consumer audio,

car sound systems, movie sound systems, audio cassettes, etc. It also manufactures some products itself.) For example, a press release from May 2002 announced that the company had sold 1 billion licensed products during its then 37 years in business. The press release also detailed the number of current licensees, breaking them down by type: media, implementation, and system hardware.

As if that weren't gold mine enough, the company posts a statistics section that further breaks down its sales (in units) by type of product such as cinema processors, AC-2 decoders, DVD-video playback units, and more, though these are cumulative rather than annual totals. The site also shows how many distributors it has and the number of countries in which it operates. Some pricing is also provided on the Web site. A Google search provides more information about licensing fees and royalty rates. With these numbers and facts, you have a good basis for estimating Dolby's revenues. For example, you will get a long way by multiplying the number of licenses by fee and royalties per license.

Although Hallmark Cards, Inc. (http://www.hallmark.com) is a private company, it announces major financials on its Web site. (Hallmark owns a public subsidiary, Crown Media Holdings, Inc., which may be the reason for the disclosure.) Start with the Press Room, then go to Corporate News. Both the company timeline and the corporate releases provide useful information.

Cost for both searches: Free.

Finding information on a private company with no financial information on its Web site: Sam Ash Music Stores

While the Web site of this privately owned chain of musical instruments and accessories stores (http://www.samash.com) provides no financial information, a quick Google search leads to a *Newsday* article from the current year that gives the company's revenue.

Cost: Free.

Australia and New Zealand

See also World.

Australian Securities and Investments Commission, http://www.asic.gov.au/asic/asic.nsf. The official company-regulating body in Australia. Name searching is free, but detailed info costs. $

CAROL, http://www.carol.co.uk. European, U.S., and Australian company annual reports.

Irasia, http://www.irasia.com. You can identify stock-exchange-listed companies in Australia, China, Hong Kong, Malaysia, Singapore, Thailand, and the U.K. Search by name, ticker symbol, industry, and/or country. Some annual reports are available. For those that are not, Irasia management will attempt to contact the company to obtain investor relations information on your behalf.

New Zealand Companies Office, http://www.companies.govt.nz. New Zealand companies, overseas companies operating in New Zealand, building societies, credit unions, and friendly societies.

New Zealand Stock Exchange, http://www.nzse.co.nz

State-Owned Enterprises from Crown Company Monitoring Advisory Unit (New Zealand), http://www.ccmau.govt.nz/soe/profiles.asp

Ireland

See also World.

Companies Registration Office, Dublin, Ireland, http://www.cro.ie. Private company information is limited. Some information is offline. $

Financial Times Annual Reports Service, http://www.annual reports.ft.com/asp/P002_search_ENG.asp. Free service providing annual reports from selected U.K., Irish, European, and North American countries.

Irion, http://www.irion.ie. Irish company profiles. Basic information is free. More detailed info runs between 30 and 50 pounds. $

Kompass Ireland, http://www.kompass.ie. Access to all financial accounts filed at the Companies Registration Office since April 1998 and reports on over 50,000 Irish companies. Reasonable prices. $

United Kingdom and Northern Ireland

See also World.

Companies House (U.K.), http://www.companies-house.gov.uk. Financial information on both live and dissolved companies. Unlike in the U.S., you can easily get private company information. Costs are reasonable for what you get. $

Company Searches and Formations, http://www.companysearches. co.uk. Financial information and documents on U.K. limited companies. $

Corporate Information, http://www.corporateinformation.com/ ukcorp.html. Metasite with links to sources for U.K. and other country company information. Also provides some information itself on more than 1,900 companies.

D & B Northern Ireland Company Database, http://www.investni.
com/mainsite/companies_search.asp?CATID=424. Details from
40,000 companies. Numerical information limited to number of
employees.

Dun & Bradstreet Small Business Centre, http://www.investni.com/
mainsite/default.asp?CATID=436. Customer reports, competitor
reports, supplier reports, partner reports for U.K. businesses.
Reasonable prices. $

Financial Times Annual Reports Service, http://www.annual
reports.ft.com/asp/P002_search_ENG.asp. Free service providing
annual reports from selected U.K., Irish, European, and North
American companies.

Hemscott, http://www.hemscott.net. U.K. company information.
Some information is free. $

Key Northern Ireland Exporters from Invest Northern Ireland,
http://www.investni.com/keyexport/index_temp.htm. Company
directory that provides numbers of employees.

List Locator, http://www.top1000.co.uk. Really a mailing list company, but you can identify companies by U.K. counties that meet
certain financial criteria. $

Northcote, http://www.northcote.co.uk. U.K. company information.
Basic information and annual reports are free. $

Northern Ireland Products Directory, http://www.investni.com/
mainsite/Product.asp?CATID=109. Company listings by product.
Numerical information limited to number of employees.

Ulster Business Online, http://www.ulsterbusiness.co.uk

U.K. Competition Commission, http://www.competition-commission. org.uk. Complaints adjudicated by the Commission may provide background information on companies, including market share.

Canada

See also World.

Canadian company search from Maplepages, http://maplepages. com/search. Sales range and number of employees.

SEDAR, http://www.sedar.com. Canadian public companies. The equivalent of the Securities and Exchange Commission in the U.S. Search by company name or industry (the latter helps you identify companies in an industry).

Europe

See also World.

Europages, http://www.europages.com. Some financials and staffing information for a wide range of European countries.

HUGIN Online International, http://www.huginonline.com. European company financial information.

Japan

Corporate Direct, http://www.c-direct.ne.jp. Annual reports of Japanese companies.

World

Bloomberg, http://www.bloomberg.com. U.S. and non-U.S. company news as well as the securities markets. Some information is free. Reasonable prices for articles. $

Corporate Information, http://www.corporateinformation.com.
Metasite covering sources from a variety of countries.

DialogSelect, http://www.dialog.com. Provides a pay-as-you-go
service. $

Financial Times, http://www.ft.com. World company financials. $

Kompass, http://www.kompass.com. Worldwide company information. Free service provides basic information. Subscription gives
you more, but you must contact the company for a quote (ugh).
Some information is free. $

LexisNexis, http://www.lexisnexis.com. Use the pay-by-credit-card
feature. Reasonable prices. Don't miss the corporate affiliations
service. $

Chapter 10

Demographics and Population Statistics

Demographics measure characteristics of human populations. Basic demographics are called *vital statistics*; they include measures of births, deaths, infant mortality, marriages, divorces, and life expectancy. Vital statistics may also include "cohabitation," number of people never married, causes of death, accidents, living arrangements of children and the elderly, child care arrangements, and average weights and heights for particular ages. Some producers broaden the term vital statistics to include not just birth, death, marriage, and living arrangements, but all kinds of basic information about populations, including health-related statistics, crime rates, ethnic identification, religious affiliation, and so on.

Demographics are often tallied by geographic or geopolitical area, such as country, region, state or province, city or metropolitan area, etc. Or they may be counted and reported by other factors. One Web site, The Right Site, http://www.easidemographics.com, even allows you to ask for a report by TV market.

How Demographic Data Are Gathered

Demographic data are gathered through the use of censuses (everyone is counted), surveys (samples), and extrapolation (projections and forecasts based on current and past data and the incorporation of information that may affect outcomes).

The major U.S. population census, the Census of Population and Housing, is taken every 10 years. Various supplementary counts are made in between, including the monthly Current Population Survey, which is based on interviews

173

of householders, and focuses on employment and unemployment; Current Employment Statistics, collected from business payrolls every month (businesses return forms to state agencies by mail, and the agencies then report to the U.S. Bureau of Labor Statistics); the Census of Manufactures, which is taken every five years (there is also an Annual Survey of Manufactures); the Census of Retail Trade; etc. Data from these periodic censuses are used to augment the basic census, covering additional subjects as well as filling in data for noncensus years. Sometimes administrative records from sources outside the Census Bureau are used for counting as well.

The decennial U.S. census is now conducted partly on a sample basis. Basic questions, such as age, marital status, race, sex, and family relationships, are asked of everyone. However, other questions, such as commute time and income, are asked of only a sample of the population.

Types of Data

Some of the types of data you can find through the sources in this chapter are:

- Birth and death rates
- Eating habits
- Education levels
- Housing patterns
- How people spend their time
- Immigration, emigration, and migration
- Income and wealth distribution
- Literacy
- Number of adherents to particular religions
- Numbers of people in particular occupations or businesses
- Population numbers and distribution
- Poverty
- Racial, ethnic, religious, age, sex, and other similar distributions
- Religious beliefs and practices

- Spending, purchasing, and saving habits
- Transportation habits

United States
General

AmeriStat, http://www.ameristat.org. U.S. population data.

CensusScope, http://www.censusscope.org. Tool for investigating U.S. demographic trends. Includes state and county rankings. Offers maps and charts.

Gateway to Census 2000 from the U.S. Census Bureau, http://www.census.gov/main/www/cen2000.html. Features news releases and other updates as more information and analysis become available.

Population Connection (formerly Zero Population Growth), http://www.populationconnection.org. Population and the environment, women's issues, health, religion, poverty, etc. Chock full of factoids.

Social Statistics Briefing Room, http://www.whitehouse.gov/fsbr/ssbr.html. Demographics, crime, health, education, income.

Statistical Abstract of the U.S., http://www.census.gov/statab/www

Children and Youth

Children Now, http://www.childrennow.org. Children and the media.

ChildStats.gov, http://childstats.gov/americaschildren. Health and well being of America's children.

Kids Count from the Annie E. Casey Foundation, http://www.aecf.org/kidscount. Disadvantaged kids in the U.S.

National Youth Violence Prevention Resource Center, http://www.safeyouth.org/home.htm. Violence by and against youth.

School District Demographics from the National Center for Education Statistics, http://nces.ed.gov/surveys/sdds. U.S. education.

Consumers

American Demographics, http://www.inside.com. Purchasing habits, attitudes, and trends. $

Surveys of Consumers, University of Michigan, http://www.sca.isr.umich.edu/main.php. Consumer sentiment, personal financial situation, attitudes about government and the economy.

Consumer attitudes: What people think about displaying the American flag

Strategy: On Google, I used the words *attitudes toward American flag.* I decided to try a search engine because it could link me to all sorts of studies and articles, though of course, I would miss articles that were only available in databases. I was not disappointed. My very first hit was a document at http://www.violence.neu.edu/September11.html called "Flag-waving as a form of self-presentation in the aftermath of September 11." The document summarized results from a poll taken by The Brudnick Center on Violence and Conflict at Northeastern University. Sixty percent of Americans were found to have displayed a flag since September 11, 2001, with 80 percent of them showing the flag outside the house, 47 percent on their car, 43 percent on clothing, 43 percent inside the house, and 21 percent in their office.

Cost: Free.

Ethnic

Asian-Nation, http://www.asian-nation.org. Asian-Americans.

Facts on the Black/African American Population from the U.S. Census Bureau, http://www.census.gov/pubinfo/www/afamhot1. html

Facts on the Hispanic/Latino Population from the U.S. Census Bureau, http://www.census.gov/pubinfo/www/hisphot1.html

Facts on the Asian American/Pacific Islander Population from the U.S. Census Bureau, http://www.census.gov/pubinfo/www/ apihot1.html

Facts on the American Indian/Alaska Native Population from the U.S. Census Bureau, http://www.census.gov/pubinfo/www/aminhot1.html

Hispanic Business, http://www.hispanicbusiness.com

Health

America's Uninsured—A Closer Look, http://www4.national academies.org/onpi/webextra.nsf/web/uninsured. Americans without health insurance.

Disability Issues Information for Journalists from The Center for an Accessible Society, http://accessiblesociety.org

Disability Statistics Center, http://www.dsc.ucsf.edu

National Center for Health Statistics, http://www.cdc.gov/nchs

Information Technology and Media

Computer Use and Ownership from the U.S. Census Bureau, http://www.census.gov/population/www/socdemo/computer.html

CyberAtlas, http://cyberatlas.internet.com. IT and Internet worldwide.

Media statistics from Mnet, http://www.media-awareness.ca/eng/issues/stats/index.htm. Canadian (and American) statistics on media usage, media content, media industries, and media issues.

Nielsen/Net Ratings, http://www.nielsen-netratings.com. U.S. and global Internet usage.

Labor

Occupational Outlook Quarterly from the U.S. Bureau of Labor Statistics, http://www.bls.gov/opub/ooq/ooqhome.htm

Occupational Outlook Handbook, http://www.bls.gov/oco. Numbers of people in occupations.

U.S. Bureau of Labor Statistics, http://www.bls.gov

Regional and Local

British Columbia Statistics, http://www.bcstats.gov.bc.ca

California Demographic Research Unit, http://www.dof.ca.gov/html/Demograp/repndat.htm. Population, immigration, migration, projections.

California Vital Statistics, http://www.dhs.cahwnet.gov/services/dhs-statistics.htm

Community Health Status Indicators Project from the U.S. Department of Health and Human Services, http://www.communityhealth.hrsa.gov

Community Information by Zip Code from the California State University Northridge University Library, http://library.csun.edu/mfinley/zipstats.html

Hawaii Vital Statistics, http://www.hawaii.gov/health

National Association of Counties, http://www.naco.org. U.S. counties.

Neighborhood Information from Yahoo!, http://list.realestate.yahoo.com/re/neighborhood/main.html

The Right Site, http://www.easidemographics.com. Economic profiles of cities, counties, states, regions, zip codes, etc.

State Data Center Program, http://www.census.gov/sdc/www. Metasite linking to U.S. state data centers.

State Fact Sheets from the Economic Research Service of the U.S. Department of Agriculture, http://www.ers.usda.gov/statefacts

State Health Facts Online from The Henry Kaiser Family Foundation, http://www.statehealthfacts.kff.org

U.S. Census Bureau Population Estimates, http://eire.census.gov/popest/estimates.php

U.S. Census Bureau State and County Quick Facts, http://quickfacts.census.gov/qfd/index.html

Vital Records Information United States, http://vitalrec.com/index.html. Metasite listing where to obtain vital records from each state, territory, and county. Health, vital statistics, race, etc.

Religion

Adherents.com, http://www.adherents.com. U.S. and international religion statistics.

American Religion Data Archive, http://www.thearda.com. Religious demographics by U.S. state, county, metro area, or the whole country. Divided into church members and adherents.

American Religious Identification Survey from The City University of New York, http://www.gc.cuny.edu/studies/aris_index.htm

The U.S. Congregational Life Survey: A National and International Study of Congregations, http://www.uscongregations.org

Miscellaneous

The Best Places to Live from CNNMoney, http://money.cnn.com/best/bplive

Urban Mobility Study from the Texas Transportation Institute, http://mobility.tamu.edu. Covers mobility and traffic congestion in 75 U.S. cities.

Voting and Registration Data from the U.S. Census Bureau, http://www.census.gov/population/www/socdemo/voting.html

Australia and New Zealand

Australian Institute of Health and Welfare, http://www.aihw.gov.au/index.html. Young people, physical activity, assisted conception, and health.

Australian Population Association, http://www.gisca.adelaide.edu.au/apa

Business Demographics from Statistics New Zealand, http://www. stats.govt.nz/domino/external/web/prod_serv.nsf/htmldocs/Business +Demographics. People and households, business and economy.

Injury Prevention Research Unit, New Zealand, http://www.otago. ac.nz/ipru/home.html

Labour Market Policy Group New Zealand, http://www.lmpg.govt. nz/bulletin.htm

New Zealand Ministry of Health, http://www.moh.govt.nz/moh.nsf? OpenDatabase

New Zealand Ministry of Social Development, http://www.mosp. govt.nz. Children, older people, families, employment, benefits, assistance programs, etc.

New Zealand Immigration Service, http://www.immigration.govt.nz/ index.html

New Zealand Office of Ethnic Affairs, http://www.ethnicaffairs. govt.nz/oeawebsite.nsf

New Zealand Work and Income, http://www.winz.govt.nz/index.html

New Zealand Health Information Service, http://www.nzhis.govt. nz/stats/statscontents.html

New Zealand Treasury, http://www.treasury.govt.nz. Income distribution.

Quality of Life in Big Cities of New Zealand, http://www.bigcities. govt.nz/index.htm

Retirement Commission of New Zealand, http://www.sorted.org. nz/demo_trends.php. Inheritance, savings, demographic trends.

Statistical Sources: New Zealand from the University of Auckland Library, http://www2.auckland.ac.nz/lbr/stats/nz_pacific/NZsources.htm

Sixty-four percent of persons in Australia 16 and over who have Internet access actually use the Internet. This figure is the same as that for the U.S., Norway, and New Zealand. The top performing country was Sweden with 78 percent in September of 2001, the most recent date measured.

Source: National Office for the Information Economy.
Strategy: Went to http://itt.dcita.gov.au/index.htm and selected Site Map, then Information Economy Statistics, then State of Play Report.
Cost: Free.

Canada

Alberta Economic Development, http://www.alberta-canada.com/index.html

CARDMedia, http://www.cardmedia.com. Population by metropolitan area and age, retail sales by metro area.

Electric Library Canada, http://www.elibrary.ca. $

Environics Research Group, http://erg.environics.net. Consumer opinion.

GDSourcing Research and Retrieval, http://www.gdsourcing.com/index.htm. Huge Canadian statistics metasite from a business research firm. You can purchase a reasonably priced guide for small business research as well.

Manitoba Industry, Trade & Mines, http://www.gov.mb.ca/itm/index.html. Includes community profiles.

New Brunswick, http://www.gnb.ca/nbfirst/e

Newfoundland. Government of Newfoundland & Labrador, http://www.nfstats.gov.nf.ca

Northwest Territories Bureau of Statistics, http://www.stats.gov.nt.ca

Saskatchewan Bureau of Statistics, http://www.gov.sk.ca/bureau.stats

Nova Scotia Finance-Statistics Division, http://www.gov.ns.ca/finance/statistics/agency

Ontario Community Profiles, http://204.101.2.101/communities/home.asp

Prince Edward Island. Government of Prince Edward Island, http://www.gov.pe.ca

Quebec. Institut de la Statistique du Quebec, http://www.stat.gouv.qc.ca. Quebec statistics.

Toronto Board of Trade, http://www.gtabot.com. Toronto area statistics.

Yukon Bureau of Statistics, http://www.gov.yk.ca/depts/eco/stats/index.html

Ireland

Central Statistics Office Ireland, http://www.cso.ie

United Kingdom and Northern Ireland

Area Report Service, http://www.areadata.co.uk/index.html. U.K. census, demographic, and market information for "any location in the U.K." Some reports are free. $

South Wales Demographics from Cardiff & Newport Call Centre Initiative, http://www.callcentrewales.co.uk

U.K. National Statistics, http://www.statistics.gov.uk

In the U.K. in 2000, men in all occupations earned nearly twice as much per week as women: 410 pounds vs. 233 pounds.

Source: Skillsbase Labour Market Information Database
Strategy: Went to http://www.skillsbase.dfes.gov.uk, selected Database, then Earnings.
Cost: Free.

World

PopNet, http://www.popnet.org. Population metasite covering the globe. Includes governmental, association, university, directory, listserv, and database sources.

Population Reference Bureau, http://www.prb.org. Worldwide information on education, employment, families, income, mortality, urbanization, race, youth, older population, and more.

Population Research Institute, http://www.pop.psu.edu/
Demography/demography.htm. Metasite listing demographic and
population sites around the world.

UCLA Center for East Asian Studies, http://www.isop.ucla.edu/eas/
Resource.htm

United Nations Population Information Network,
http://www.un.org/ popin

World Population Trends from the U.N. Population Division
Department of Economic and Social Affairs, http://www.un.org/
popin/wdtrends.htm

Chapter 11

Special Tips and Tricks

In this chapter you will find a collection of tips both interesting and quirky. Read on to find out about:

- Determining what things cost
- Estimating your competitor's marketing costs
- How to use media kits, interview transcripts, and company filings to find out about industries
- How to use government statistics to get a foothold in a topic
- Knowing the right questions to ask

Cost of Labor

Knowing the cost of labor for your staff or proposed staff will help you write business plans, budget, and hire effectively. It will also help you estimate your competitors' costs.

Use these sites to determine salaries, benefits, and other compensation for workers in your geographical area. Be sure to check the world sources as well as those specific to your country:

United States

Computerjobs.com, http://www.computerjobs.com/homepage.aspx

JobStar, http://jobstar.org/index.cfm/. Sponsored by libraries in the state of California, this excellent site links to more than 300 salary surveys on the Web. Also links to cost of living surveys for the U.S. in general and California specifically.

Occupational Outlook Handbook, http://www.bls.gov/oco. Pay for people in various occupations.

Australia

National Remuneration Centre (Australia), http://www.natrem. com.au. Pay rates and links to salary surveys. $

SalaryZone, http://www.salaryzone.com.au. Salaries in Australia. Information technology, banking, finance, accounting, and office support.

Wage$.com.au, http://www.wages.com.au. Wages in Australia. Also links to other salary sites around the world.

Canada

Canadian Labour Market Information, http://lmi-imt.hrdc-drhc. gc.ca. Salaries and employment levels.

Ireland

Executive Salaries in Ireland, http://www.ireland.com/jobs/advice/ salary.htm

Jobs in Ireland, http://www.topjobs.ie. Irish salaries.

Russia

Salary Survey Report from Meteor Personnel (Russia), http://www.meteor.ru. Russian salaries. $

United Kingdom and Northern Ireland

Regional U.K. Salary Calculator, http://www.reed.co.uk/cgi-bin/calculator.asp

SalarySearch, http://www.salarysearch.co.uk. U.K. salaries and benefits. $

World

Salary.com, http://www.salary.com. Search for jobs, then see what the pay is. Works for the U.S., Canada, the U.K., Asia, and India. Other areas covered, but sparsely.

Salary Expert, http://www.salaryexpert.com. International.

Cost of Real Estate

You need to know the cost of real estate when planning for new locations and employee relocation. You'll also want to know how good a deal you're getting.

United States

CoStar Group, http://www.costar.com. U.S. real estate. Building-specific information on 800,000 properties, including comparable sales, cap rates, income and expense data, lease expirations, and loan terms. Covers "virtually every building in every major city" and six million tenants, owners and brokers. General market trends are free. $

Grubb & Ellis, http://www.grubb-ellis.com. U.S. Market Trends is Grubb & Ellis's quarterly report on national market conditions, including the office, industrial, retail, multihousing, and telecom markets.

Realtor.com, http://www.realtor.com. U.S. home prices.

Realtor.org, http://www.realtor.org. U.S. home prices by metro area and state, apartment/condo/co-op prices by state, housing affordability index, etc.

Canada

e-Space Connections, http://www.e-space.com/homeindex.cfm. Canadian commercial real estate.

Royal LePage, http://www.royallepage.com. Canadian office and commercial property.

World

CB Richard Ellis, http://www.cbrichardellis.com. Office rents, vacancy rates, and occupancy costs worldwide.

Collier's International Market Reports, http://www.colliers.com/fr_market.html. Real estate around the world. Some information is a bit old, but much is quite usable.

Cushman & Wakefield, http://www.cushmanwakefield.com/globhome.html. Real estate market summaries around the world.

Oncor International, http://www.oncorintl.com/Default.asp?bhcp=1. European and North American office property reports plus South Africa, Mexico, and Brazil.

Case Study: What things cost: Cost of government regulation on small business

Purpose: This case study demonstrates how to find out what things cost.

Sources: Google

I decided to use Google because it is such a good starting point. My strategy was *"cost of government regulation" small business.* By making "cost of government regulation" a phrase, I thought I would focus the search and minimize the number of irrelevant hits. I was not disappointed. My very first hit led to an article on Microsoft bcentral.com, a site for its small business solutions, called "Warning: Government Regulations Ahead" (www.bcentral.com/articles/harper109.asp?format=print). The article reported the findings of several organizations that studied the issue, including the National Federation of Independent Business (NFIB), which found that the average cost for complying with government regulation came to an average of $125,000 per business. In addition, the Office of Management and Budget estimated that every year, 300 federal regulations are passed that cost the economy at least $125 million each.

Another Google hit led me to a study by the Small Business Administration at http://www.sba.gov/advo/research/rs207tot.pdf that gave further information. For example, firms employing fewer than 20 employees spend $6,975 annually per employee to comply with regulations. About 40 percent of this cost relates to environmental and tax paperwork and compliance.

Lessons Learned

✔   Phrase searching is a powerful and useful tool.

✔   You can find PDF files using Google.

✔   It can be surprisingly easy to answer seemingly complex questions.

Case Study: How much does enterprise data storage cost?

Purpose: This case study demonstrates how to use an industry Web site to find out what things cost.

Sources: Computerworld.

I decided to try a computer site like Computerworld at http://www.computerworld.com or C/NET at http://www.cnet.com or Ziff-Davis at http://www.zdnet.com. I never got beyond the first one.

At Computerworld, I chose the advanced search capability because it gave me good control over dates and sentence construction. My strategy was:

- Should contain in the body the phrase: *enterprise storage*
- And must contain in the body the words: *cost*
- And should contain in the body the words: *gigabyte* in the last 90 days.

This strategy was designed to unearth sentences like "Enterprise storage costs $n per gigabyte." Lo and behold, I found an article from the previous day entitled "The Incredible Shrinking Storage Media" that states, "HAMR [heat-assisted magnetic recording technology] could take the cost of disk storage, now at about $1 per gigabyte, to 10 cents in five years ..."

There are various types of storage, some irrelevant to my question, but the article is about enterprise storage, though it never uses the word "enterprise." I found this article because my first specification said that the article *should* contain the phrase "enterprise storage" rather than that it *must* contain it. (Actually, that was a mistake. I had meant to say "must contain," but somehow the drop-down menu exerted its will and I missed it. Just to see what would happen, I repeated the search with "must contain" and my article was missing. None of the articles included in this batch held my answer, so I was lucky. Had I executed this search in the first place, missing my article, I would have had to expand the date range and/or try other search terms or another source.)

Lessons Learned

✔   An article can be right on target without using the terminology you expect.

✔   Industry Web sites are powerful sources of information.

✔   Advanced search features give you good control over your search.

Marketing Costs

Finding out what a company spends on marketing can be surprisingly easy. Public companies often list sales and marketing expenses as a line item in their filings with the Securities and Exchange Commission. Those numbers give you a starting point. By knowing something about how the company distributes its products, you can make an educated guess about the proportions of sales to marketing expenses. For example, if a company has many sales offices, it has an expensive sales force. If it goes through distributors, its sales expenses are lower because the distributors take care of the selling. If the company only sells direct through its Web site and/or a catalog, its sales expenses will be low. (The real expense comes from a sales force that goes out and calls on potential customers.)

You can often find out about marketing costs from media. For example, a Google search on *"marketing budget" Microsoft xbox* immediately leads to an article from news.com that announces a $500 million launch cost for the Xbox. Another article in the hit list puts that in perspective by saying "Microsoft says that its marketing for the Xbox has been the largest effort ever for one of its products. In fact, the Xbox's marketing budget is the largest for any game console in history, easily surpassing Sega's $100 million campaign in 1998."

You can also estimate a company's marketing budget if you know its total revenues. Companies typically spend about a third of their revenues on marketing, so if you know total revenue, you can take a good guess. By exploring the amount of buzz the company is generating, looking at its marketing and advertising strategies (trade show appearances, television, print ads, etc.), and checking out retailer shelves if the product is sold through stores, you can get a feel for whether the company is spending a lot or a little on marketing. Sometimes letters to shareholders, annual reports, and other investor information will tell you whether the company intends to expand or pull back on its marketing efforts. For public companies, you can compare the salary of the VP of Marketing, found in the executive compensation portion of the 10-K, with those of others to see how much the company values its marketing personnel.

For example, this item from Adobe's 2001 10-K tells us that the company spends a healthy percentage of its revenue on marketing: "We believe our future success will depend in part on our continued ability to recruit and retain highly skilled technical, management and marketing personnel." This company values its marketing staff as much as its technical personnel.

In the financial section of the 10-K we find the following:

Figures in millions	2001	Change 2000	2000	Change 1999	1999
Sales and marketing	$403.7	0.6%	$401.2	22%	$328.5
Percentage of total revenue	32.8%		31.7%		32.3%

Indeed, Adobe's marketing budget, or at least its *sales* and marketing budget, comes very close to a third of its revenues.

The company goes on to say that it is increasing this budget: "As communicated on December 13, 2001, for the first quarter of fiscal 2002, our sales and marketing expense target is approximately 34–35% of revenue. For fiscal year 2002, we are targeting such expenditures also to be approximately 34–35% of revenue."

Note that the company wraps sales and marketing into one line item, which makes it difficult to separate them. However, what is the purpose of estimating a company's marketing budget in the first place? To get a good idea of how aggressively it is promoting its products and to see where those products are being promoted. You don't *have* to separate out sales and marketing expenses in order to get an overall feel for these issues. You may be able to get pieces of the picture from the 10-K, annual report, and press releases, such as this sentence, also from Adobe's 10-K: "Advertising costs for fiscal years 2001, 2000, and 1999 were $30.5 million, $32.9 million, and $22.4 million, respectively." See Chapter 12 on estimating techniques for more hints on calculating companies' expenses.

Using Media Kits

Media kits can help you determine the best marketing channels for reaching your target market. For example, the media kit for *Business Week*, http://mediakit.businessweek.com, tells us that of North American small business subscribers (225,000 of them), 88 percent are male. That means that if we want to reach women in small business, we would probably do better advertising elsewhere. This use of media kits is the traditional one.

However, there's more you can do with them:

- Identify competitors and their characteristics. Digital Media Net's kit, http://www.digitalmedianet.com, tells you which Web sites and newsletters for digital creatives it considers its competition, at least the ones it thinks it beats in the numbers game.

- Determine industry size. The media kit for *Engineering News-Record*, http://www.enr.com/media_kit/index.asp, tells us that construction is a $3.4-plus trillion industry, and *Publishers Weekly*, http://www.publishers weekly.com, tells us that the book industry rakes in $23 billion worldwide per year. *Drug Discovery & Development* at http://www.dddmag.com provides a list of the top 20 pharm/biotech companies and their R & D spending for the latest year available.

You can also estimate the size of an industry, even if the media kit doesn't give you the specific number. Here's a trick to try: Look at the circulation figures for various journals in a particular field. You will quickly be able to tell which are the major journals and which are the minor ones. Add the figures for the various journals together, and to account for overlapping readerships, take about 75 percent of the total. This figure is not the total market size in users, but the number of readers you can reach through those channels—a starting point for estimating total industry size as measured in users or units sold.

Most people in a particular field do not read journals, which means that the total market size is quite a bit larger than your figure. To the circulation figures, you can add trade show attendance and the sizes of relevant Internet communities. Be sure once again to compensate for overlap.

Estimating beyond that will be tricky because you don't know how much of the industry these figures represent. You will have to guess based on other information you have about the industry, but at least now you have a good diving board from which to plunge.

Using 10-Ks and Annual Reports

You can find a surprising amount of useful industry information as well as insight into the company itself by looking at its government filings and annual

---

Unit sales of a company's product using interview transcripts

Pinnacle Systems sold about half a million low-end video editing systems in a recent quarter.

Source: *The Wall Street Transcript*, http://www.twst.com

Strategy: I clicked on Archive. I then typed *pinnacle* in the search box and specified that items should be dated later than January 1, 2002. That got me an interview with Mark Sanders, CEO. A short excerpt is free. The entire article is available only to subscribers, who must pay $195 per quarter for the publication's Consumer Focus feature.

Note: Because the free excerpts don't include the interview date, be sure you search a narrow date range so that you know about when the interview took place.

---

reports. Of course, the amount of information will vary by company and by publication. For example:

- Microsoft's letter to shareholders gives us the number of PCs in the world and forecasts the number to be sold during the next year: "More than 500 million PCs are already in use around the world, and another 130 million or more will be purchased in calendar 2001—more than the number of TVs that will likely be purchased this year."

- Microsoft's 10-K provides the company's sales and marketing expenses in real and percentage terms, and also breaks down the number of employees by general function (R & D, sales and marketing, support, manufacturing and distribution, and finance and administration). It also specifies the number of employees in and outside the U.S. as well as the number of square feet at many of its sites. You can estimate the number of employees at each site by determining the type of facility it is (office, manufacturing) and dividing the square footage by the typical number of square feet per person (150 to 200 square feet per office worker).

It's unusual to find unit sales in a 10-K, but you might be able to find such numbers either in the annual report or in the press and marketing materials on the company's Web site. In some cases you can estimate them yourself (see Chapter 12 for techniques). Some companies break down financials by subsidiary or division, and some do not. Most companies offer some kind of breakdown by general product category/operating unit.

Using Government Figures
Population Estimates

The U.S. Census Bureau publishes population estimates and projections between its decennial censuses, which take place in years ending in zero. Every time a new estimate is published, all years back to the previous census are revised. Methodology for estimates consists of incorporating vital statistics (birth and death) and immigration figures from agencies like the National Center for Health Statistics and the Immigration and Naturalization Service (INS). Projections are based on alternative assumptions for future fertility, life expectancy, net international migration, and (for state-level projections) state-to-state or domestic migration. Both estimates and projections are produced at the national, state, and local levels.

You can use population figures for a variety of purposes. For example, the list of 100 fastest-growing counties linked from http://eire.census.gov/popest/estimates.php might help you make relocation decisions, though of course, you will need to do in-depth research, including in-person visits, before you can make a final decision. Changes in births, deaths, and migrations by state can also help you decide where to locate and/or market and sell your products. Projections by age will indicate how big the teenage girl or over-65 markets will be over the next few years.

Other Census Bureau Information

The U.S. Census Bureau provides a wealth of information about not only the population, but also business (e.g., manufacturing and retail sales), assets of state and local governments (useful if you want to sell something to them), transportation, foreign trade, and agriculture. Consult the subject index to Census Bureau data linked from the main page at http://www.census.gov.

The *Statistical Abstract of the U.S.*, which is also linked from the Census Bureau main page, is the gold standard of U.S. government statistical publications. Drawing from not only government, but also private sources of statistics, the *Abstract* provides information on population, industry and business, natural resources, health, recreation, labor, transportation, information and communication, foreign commerce and aid, financial services, economic indicators, and the legal and political systems. Information tends to be general, meaning you won't find exact specific market sizes, but you can get good ballpark figures from which to work.

For example, you can find out how much consumers spend on various healthcare items like hospitals, doctor visits, drugs, insurance, and nursing homes. Check out the cost of living index for selected metropolitan areas. See what the penetration of cable television is. Find out how many college graduates watch prime time television. Learn how much consumers spend on jewelry.

Consumer Spending and Demographics

The U.S. Bureau of Labor Statistics produces consumer expenditure reports that can be very useful to businesspeople. The Consumer Expenditure Survey is published every year and is based on quarterly interviews and diaries. Go to the Bureau's home page at http://www.bls.gov and select "Consumer Expenditures." Once there, you have several choices, but if you want something specific, it is well worth selecting the "Get detailed statistics" link, then one of the "Create custom tables" links. From there, you can select any of a large number of individual categories, such as alcoholic beverages, footwear, beef, furniture, public transportation, electricity, and income taxes. You can then specify that you want to see spending in that area by age, income, geographic region, occupation, origin, education, size of family, family composition, and so on.

Following is an extended case study that involves starting with the agency's collection, then doing some estimating on our own plus some further searching.

Extended Case Study: What Do People of Certain Ages Spend on Entertainment Fees and Admissions?

Purpose: This case study demonstrates how to find consumer spending figures using government and association data and how to extrapolate from them.

Sources: Bureau of Labor Statistics and Motion Picture Association of America Web sites

From the Bureau of Labor Statistics custom table as described previously, we select:

> Entertainment fees and admissions
>
> Age of reference person

We can build up all ages by selecting one age range at a time and clicking on "Add to your selection." When we do so, we build up multiple queries. Once we have added queries for all age ranges, we click on "Get Data," and our table pops up in a separate browser window. The system gives us separate tables for each age range and provides 10 years' worth of data. We are only interested in the latest year, so we select "Change Output Options," set the starting year to the current year, and hit "Go." Now we can see what each age range spends on entertainment admissions. For the latest year available, which is 2000, people spend the following number of dollars:

Age	
Under 25	$271
25–34	460
35–44	715
45–54	637
55–64	509
65–74	416
Over 75	214

These data are a bit surprising. After all, the common wisdom is that consumers from 18 to 35 spend the most money going to the movies and concerts. Then why does this survey show that it is consumers between 35 and 64 who spend the most on entertainment admissions?

The secret lies in the definitions. The spending that is being measured here is by consumer unit, not per individual. It is the age of the reference person, that is, the first member of the consumer unit mentioned by the survey respondent, that is being used. Therefore, these data do not mean that people between the ages of 35 and 64 spend the most on entertainment admissions for themselves only, the data mean that people between those ages (those most likely to have children at home) spend the most per household!

The way to determine spending per capita is this:

1) Take the number of consumer units in the survey.

2) Multiply the average annual expenditure on entertainment admissions by the number of consumer units to get the total spending on entertainment.

3) Multiply the number of consumer units by the average number of persons in each unit to get the total number of consumers in the survey.

4) Divide the total spending by the number of consumers to get spending per consumer per year.

If you follow these directions, be sure to use the correct source material. The first time I performed these calculations, I took the line item "Entertainment" from the 2000 Consumer Expenditure Survey, average annual expenditures of all consumer units and percent changes. That was a mistake. The entertainment expenditure figures there included not just admissions and fees, but other types of entertainment as well, and yet there was no way to tell that by looking at the tables. When my intrepid editor, John Bryans, questioned my figures, I discovered the error. Be sure to use the data from the Current Standard Tables and pick up the figures for fees and admissions only.

These calculations give us the average entertainment admission spending per person per year, but they don't tell us the average per person by age. In fact, there is no way to determine this information from the Consumer Expenditure Survey because we don't know the age distribution of the individuals in the survey, only those of the reference persons for each consumer unit (probably heads of household, more or less).

To get at this information, let's try entertainment industry sources. The Motion Picture Association of America ought to track such things. Sure enough, when I go to its site at http://www.mpaa.org, I follow a link to "U.S. Economic Reviews" and find what I'm looking for. In a 2001 attendance study, there is a chart of movie attendance by age that shows that 47 percent of moviegoers are under the age of 30. (The chart breaks down attendance into age ranges. I have added together the youngest four ranges to come up with the 47 percent.) People over 50 account for only 17 percent of moviegoers, while adults between 30 and 49 account for 36 percent of the audience. Another table tells me that 12- to 24-year-olds account for 40 percent of frequent moviegoers. So you see, the common wisdom was correct after all—despite the fact that we still can't tell exactly which age group spends the most money without adjusting for ticket prices. Whether frequency of attendance is an issue depends on the definition of moviegoer. Is one admission equal to one moviegoer? If so, you don't need to adjust for frequency of attendance. If not, you might have to.

Lessons Learned

✔ Statistics aren't always grouped the way you want them. You may have to combine existing data and/or extrapolate from them.

✔ Definitions are critical. If you don't understand what is being counted and how, you can draw erroneous conclusions.

> ✔ Use what you know about an industry to find likely sources of information. In this case, we knew enough to guess that the Motion Picture Association of America would track movie attendance and spending.
>
> ✔ You often have to bring in information from a variety of sources in order to answer a question.
>
> ✔ Use your own excellent brain to extrapolate from the figures you are able to find.
>
> ✔ Verify, verify, verify!

Knowing the Right Questions to Ask

Some questions simply cannot be answered as posed. However, you often can get at the information by asking alternative questions.

For example, say I want to know how many amateur filmmakers there are. There is no direct way to answer the question because no one tracks how many amateurs make films. However, we can estimate the answer by finding out what amateur filmmakers do that *can* be counted. One of those things is their purchases.

It's pretty difficult to be a filmmaker of any kind without a camera, so we can assume that each amateur has a camera. In some cases, the cameras will be rented or borrowed, but many will be purchased. In addition, many of them will be video rather than film cameras because video is much more affordable than film, which is exorbitantly expensive. Therefore, we might be able to approximate a figure by counting the number of digital video cameras purchased and estimating the portion sold to amateur filmmakers rather than, say, people who make home or vacation videos.

Filmmakers don't shoot their projects straight through—they have to edit, so it is safe to say that another way of getting at this information is by counting units of video editing software sold. Much of that is bundled with new computers and never used, so if we select this measure we'll have to adjust for that. Some video editing software is bundled with camcorders and also never utilized.

If we can separate the bundled software from units actually purchased, we'll have a good start.

You can see where I'm going with this idea. If you can't get at the thing directly, find some oblique door that leads to the answer.

Other helpful things besides purchases you can count include:

- Magazine circulations
- Trade show attendance
- Web community sizes
- Association memberships
- Concert, sport, theater, or movie attendance
- Number of travelers
- People with certain diseases or conditions
- People in certain age, geographical, sex, ethnic, etc. brackets

None of these measures ever represents all the people who are interested in a subject, but they can provide a starting place. I have seen no formulas for estimating the number of people who do something but don't read the magazines/go to the trade shows/join things, so you will have to make educated guesses about the total size of each group.

Chapter 12

Your Competitive Advantage: Estimating Company Numbers You Can't Get

Despite the wonders of the Web, we all know how difficult it still can be in this day and age to find the statistics you want. However, there is help for frustrated seekers. It is possible to estimate basic numerical information about companies, markets, and other things when you can't find firm statistics about them. Of course, the more information you have as a starting point, the better, but you can accomplish a surprising amount with just a small toehold. It's important to understand that this method will yield educated guesses only and that you won't always be able to verify your numbers. However, if you follow the company or industry over time, you will be able to pick up additional clues and refine your model.

While this chapter focuses on information you can estimate about companies, you can use the same techniques to estimate other kinds of statistics. Read on to explore the types of company information you can estimate, and what you need to derive your desired figures, techniques, sources, and examples.

What You Can Estimate About a Private Company or Division of a Public Company

Some of the major company benchmarks you can estimate are:

- Revenue
- Units sold
- Costs, including marketing expenses, staff costs, operations
- Whether profitable
- Market size for a product

Preliminary Information You Will Need

Proper estimating requires that you know at least something about the target company and its industry segment. Obviously, the more you know, the better off you are.

- To determine *revenues and units sold,* find out where the company is in its life cycle, how it is funded, market size, type of products, price of products, distribution channels, number of locations, target market, timeline, number of employees.
- To determine *market size,* find out how the company markets, who its competitors are, its products, distribution channels, product prices, target market.
- To determine *market share,* find out about competitors, buzz, timeline.
- To determine *costs,* find out how the company markets, who its competitors are, number of facilities, number of employees, type of employees, location, market size, distribution channels, target market, timeline.
- To determine *whether the company is profitable,* find out how it is funded, startup date, distribution channels, products, product prices, timeline, number of employees, how marketed.

The basic steps for gathering this information are:

1. Draw up a timeline.

2. Find out or infer how the company is funded.

3. Look at the company's products and how they are sold.

4. Look at the company's target market.

5. Use what you know about the industry.

6. Find out about competitors.

7. Look at how the company markets its products.

8. Evaluate how much buzz the company gets.

As you work, you will go back and forth among these steps. Don't worry about repetition. It's part of the process.

The following sections explain how to obtain this information. But first, you will need to understand the types of companies there are and how they are funded.

Step One: Timeline

A timeline is your most important tool. It will tell you:

- Whether the company is a startup (and whether it should have sales)
- How the company is funded
- Whether the company's products are successful
- Something about marketing costs
- Likely maximum annual revenues and growth possibilities for the next two years

The first point on your timeline should be date of founding. As you go through the other steps, you can add to your timeline.

By determining how long the company has been in business, you can tell where it is in its lifecycle. If it's been around for more than about three years—maybe as much as five, it may have products and sales—it certainly ought to. If it has sales, it has marketing costs. If the company is more than three years old and has no products, it is probably not in good shape. If it is venture-capital (VC) funded, the investors will have lost confidence by now. If it is owner-funded, it is either a hobby or the owner has deep pockets.

Sources for determining the date of founding include:

- Corporate filings with the secretary of state, if a U.S. company. If a U.K. company, go to Companies House for official documents.
- The company's Web site. Press releases may include announcements of funding rounds. The "About" section may also be helpful.
- Articles.

Step Two: Funding

Find out or infer how the company is funded. This information will help you determine whether the company is profitable, or at least meeting its targets. Each type of company has a particular life cycle. If you know where it is in that cycle, you can infer something about sales, costs, and profitability.

In order to understand how the company is funded, you need to know something about types of companies:

- **Founder-funded.** In this type of company, the founder puts in his or her own money and perhaps that of friends and relatives. To make the company grow, the founder either bootstraps (continually reinvests the profits from revenues) or grows the company just enough to make it attractive to investors or acquirers. Some founders want to run the company indefinitely. In this case, the company is known as a lifestyle company. Others want to make money and get out through either a trade sale or a public offering. Founder-funded companies range in age from startup to mature company.

- **Angel-funded.** This type of company is funded by wealthy individual investors who typically put in $100,000 or more early in the company's life cycle. In the past, angel investors took on the role of benefactors, patiently funding product development and willing to wait for revenues to come in, but in today's harsh economic climate, angel investors have become much more like venture capitalists: strict, hard-nosed, risk-averse investors who want to see firm customers or real revenues before investing. Angels used to fund lifestyle companies, taking profit in the form of dividends, but now they want companies to achieve an exit (trade sale or go public) so they can cash out. Angel-funded companies range in age from startup to mature company, though increasingly less of the latter.

- **Venture-funded (early, mid- and late-stage).** Venture capitalists (VCs) are demanding investors who expect huge, quick returns on their money. Unlike angels, they do not represent themselves, but manage funds made up of other people's money. In the past, this type of investor started with new companies by putting in small amounts of money, then larger amounts as the company grew, assuming it met its milestones and could assure the investors it was on the right track. However, VCs are now coming in at later and later stages to avoid early-stage risk. (There has also traditionally been later stage VC investment.) Like newer angel-funded companies, venture-funded companies grow and achieve an exit, or they fail. If you come across a venture-funded company, it is probably at most five years old. However, late-stage venture funding is used to grow an already successful company that has great potential.

- **Public.** We all know about public companies. They are stockholder-funded and must report financial and operational information to their stockholders and the public. There is a lot of information available about them, although detailed information is sometimes hard to get. For example, it can be difficult to obtain specific information about a division or subsidiary or measures like numbers of units sold. You can use the same estimating techniques on both private and public companies. Public companies are usually more than three years old, though during the Internet boom, they were often younger, growing faster than normally required to make a public offering.

Knowing whether a company is angel-, venture-, or founder-funded will indicate where it is in its life cycle and how much confidence investors have in it. Be careful in your assumptions, however. Just because a company was founded in a particular year (see Step 1) does not necessarily mean that the founder worked for it full-time or really got it going immediately. However, if it is venture-funded, you know that the company had to spring into action and there is serious full-time work going on. Venture-funded companies get started right away because the investors are constantly on management's back.

The best source for determining funding is the company's Web site:

- Look for press releases. If you can tell who the company's VCs are, you can also check the VCs' Web sites for press releases about the companies in which they invest. You might be able to tell how much has been invested and whether the company is profitable.
- Check to see if the company has products or services. If not and it has been around more than three to five years, it is probably not venture-funded. VCs would have closed it up by now if there were no sales.
- Find out who started and is running the company. A Mom and Pop operation is probably self-financed.

Step Three: Products and Services

Look at the company's products or services, including how they are sold and how long they have been on the market. This information will tell you:

- Revenues
- Market size
- Implications for profitability (margin)

First, determine whether the company has products or services at all. If it does, it probably has sales. If the company is new and the products are very expensive, it may not have sales yet because of the long lead-time needed for commitment from customers; capital expenses often require board approval. If it is very unlucky or not well run, it may have products and no sales simply because no one wants to buy what it is selling. However, if it has products or services for sale, you know that it is beyond the early startup stage, although it may still be tiny.

If the company has no products or services, it is living on investment or borrowed money and is relatively new. You can verify this conclusion by consulting its corporate filings as mentioned previously. If the company has been around for a while, the founders are either running the business part time, financing it themselves, or both. They may also be working with money from "friends and family." In this case, the company is not market-driven and is probably suffering from poor management. It may be headed by a techie or some other evangelist.

If the company has products or services to offer, it will probably have a sales staff unless its only sales channels are direct selling over the Web or resellers. The presence of a sales staff implies that the company is not tiny, though it may be on the small side.

Sources for product information include:

- The company's Web site.

- Live research. Call the company and ask the price of the product or where you can buy it. If no one will tell you, you can be fairly certain the company has no products and no sales and is probably very small. (If it is a technology licensing company, the technology is tantamount to a product.)

After you have looked at the products or services themselves, determine how the company distributes them. This information helps tell you what the margin is and how big the company is.

If it sells direct, its margin will be greater than if it goes through distributors and retail outlets. If it has distributors, the company will be smaller than if it sells direct (unless it is selling only through its Web site). For software companies, distribution may tell you something about company size. If the company sells software by electronic download, it has to be selling a significant number of units. Electronic software download (ESD) companies that do fulfillment will not handle small volumes. ESD companies charge about 20 percent, which means that the company is netting 80 percent of the retail price. Retailers take 50 percent of the retail price.

Sources for distribution information include:

- The company's Web site. Look for press releases or "Where you can buy this product."

- Live research. Call the company and ask where you can buy the product. Call resellers and see if they have the product. Do they stock the item regularly? Do they sell many of it? If it requires a special order, they are not likely to be selling any.

Next, determine how long the product has been on the market. This information will tell you whether it is successful, since unsuccessful products fade away. Longevity also implies that a respectable number of units is being sold. The number considered "respectable" will depend on price and the company's costs. Obviously several MRI machines will yield far more revenue than the same number of washing machines.

Sources for product longevity include:

- The company's Web site. Look for press releases and product information.
- Product reviews
- Articles
- Distributors and retailers

Step Four: Target Market

Look at the company's target market. This will help you determine:

- Market size
- Maximum revenues
- Type of personnel employed

Look at the company's products to identify the target market. Is the product targeted at people who fit certain criteria? If so, how many of them are there? For example, a software product called Broadband Wizard is only of use to people who have broadband Internet access, so you need to know how many people have broadband access.

Think carefully about who would use the product. Does the product sell to every individual or household? Would a person own more than one? Would only a certain age group buy it? Look at the size of that demographic and its spending power and habits. This is the market opportunity.

Once you have determined a size for your market, use prices of products to calculate maximum sales (price times market opportunity).

Sources for market size (more information elsewhere in this book):

- Government sources, like the U.S. Bureau of Labor Statistics, Statistical Abstract, Occupational Outlook, and Census Bureau

- Associations

- Market research reports

- Articles

- Media kits for circulation of trade journals and Web sites

- Analogies and inferences. For example, people who have DSL connections also have firewalls; therefore, if *n* number of DSL residential connections exist, probably *n* firewalls have been sold to residential computer users

- Trade journal writers and editors

Step Five: Use What You Know About the Industry

You can make educated guesses about how the company operates, what its costs are, what its revenues are likely to be, and whether it is profitable. For example:

- By knowing something about the company's business, you can guess at the mix of staff roles and talents. For example, a software company needs programmers, system designers, and engineers. A bookseller needs many clerical people.

- Salaries will help determine the company's costs. Adobe's average salary will far exceed that of Starbucks. Estimate the proportion of technical, clerical, and marketing staff, and research their salaries. (See the salary sites in Chapter 11.)

- Overall market size helps determine maximum sales and market share as well as number of employees. Once you have that, proceed as follows:

- To determine market share, start from the size of major competitors using this rule of thumb: A company is thought to be doing okay if it has 5 percent of a market and well if it has 30 percent of a market. If the company is doing well, its sales should be about 30 percent of the market, possibly lower. If just so-so, its sales should be 5 percent to 10 percent, and so on. Check yourself by determining about how many competitors there are. This tells you about how many pieces in the pie and approximately how big each piece is. If you can get the competitors' sales, you are already ahead.

- For number of employees, you can make estimates based on the likely number of employees needed to generate certain amounts of revenue. Of course, these figures will vary by industry. You can get benchmarks by looking at annual reports and filings from public companies.

- Once you know the revenue, you can work backward. If you know the company is profitable or breaking even, then you know that expenses must be the same as or less than revenues. Figure that 80 percent of costs go for personnel. Estimate the mix of employees, research their salaries, and multiply the salaries by 127 percent, the additional 27 percent representing benefits. How many employees of each type could you support on that personnel budget?

- You can estimate distribution costs and gross margins by checking standard industry practice. For example, typical retail markup is 100 percent. Supermarket net margins run one to two percent. If you don't know the standards for the industry, a quick spin around with Google should sort them out for you.

Sources for employee information:

- The company's Web site may give you the number of employees. It may also tell you the types of people the company is recruiting. You can tell what phase the company is in by the types of people it is looking for. If the company is searching for senior-level people, it is probably in a growth phase and making a loss (if venture-funded).

- Get salaries from salary and compensation Web sites. See Chapter 11 for suggestions.

Step Six: Find Out About Competitors

Identifying competitors and finding out how they do business will tell you something about market share and relative sales. How the competition is faring and how it conducts itself also carries possible implications for the company's marketing budget.

You can assume, though not infallibly so, that the companies with the greatest buzz and media presence enjoy the largest market shares. Again, if you know the size of the entire industry, you can estimate those shares and the revenues of the companies in that space.

Identify competitors, their sales and buzz through:

- Product reviews
- Articles
- Hoover's Online, http://www.hoovers.com
- 10-Ks and other filings of public companies
- Trade associations
- Retailer shelves
- NASDAQ (See the company capsule, which is furnished by Hoover's)

Step Seven: Marketing

Look at how the company markets its products. This will tell you:

- Size of the marketing budget
- Implications for market size

In order to determine how the company markets, look at the following:

- Public relations. Is the company employing a PR agency? These agencies can cost $8,000 to $10,000 per month. One method of determining a PR agency's presence is to examine the contacts on the company's press releases, as well as the content of the releases where announcements of new deals may be made. Advertising trade journals also announce that such-and-such company has retained the services of so-and-so agency.

- TV commercials. If the company is advertising on television, especially in prime time, it is spending a bundle.

- Trade shows. Look at exhibitor lists for likely trade shows, then the exhibit floor map, which tells you the number of square feet for each booth. The larger the display, the more the company is spending. You can get costs from the show's management, but remember that there are always additional costs for fancy design, signage, equipment, and so on.

- Magazine advertising. How many magazines carry the company's advertisement? What size are the ads? What does the magazine charge for those ads? (Remember that discounts are offered for multiple runs and for ads placed through agencies.)

- Joint marketing. Is the company running ads or promotions together with other companies?

Step Eight: Buzz

Evaluate how much buzz the company gets in the media. This will help you guess at market share.

One method for ascertaining the pecking order of competitors is to evaluate the amount of buzz the company generates. The more buzz, the greater the marketing budget, and the greater the overall size of the company (probably about three times the size of the marketing budget).

Sources include:

- Articles
- Product reviews
- News groups, electronic discussion lists, conferences
- The number of books written about the company or its products

Putting It All Together

Once you have gathered some or all of the key information, you can estimate the following:

Number of units being sold

- Focus on products that are being sold directly rather than those bundled or sold through original equipment manufacturers (OEMs). Bundled products are heavily discounted. The company could be shipping significant volumes of products and still not making much money. Or it might. Some software companies claim that the huge volumes are allowing them to make bundles from their bundling. Be sure to differentiate between units shipped/downloaded and units actually sold. Do not take the company's claims for number of units shipped at face value. These numbers could comprise many units sold at less than profitable prices or even free giveaways.

- Work backward from the revenues you have estimated and the prices of the products. Divide revenues by prices.

- Reviews and knowledge of competitors will help you guess which products are selling best so you can weight them more heavily.

The company's costs

Subtract costs from revenues to get net income. To calculate the company's costs, you should do one or all of the following:

- Determine the company's number of locations
- Determine personnel costs
- Figure overhead costs
- Estimate marketing costs
- Estimate capital costs

The *number of locations* a company has will help tell you:

- Number of employees. If the company has many locations, there is at least one sales person and one overhead person at each.

- Proportion of sales people. More locations imply more sales people, and sales people are highly paid.

- Overhead costs. Each facility adds to overhead.

Sources for number of locations include:

- Company Web site, including press releases
- Annual reports and filings
- Trade show presentations
- Articles

Personnel costs will help you learn whether the company is running at a loss. See Step 6 for calculating numbers of employees and their costs. Once you determine the costs, you can tell if the revenues support that level of staffing. If not, the company is running at a loss.

Overhead costs also help ascertain profitability. Overhead typically runs 20 percent of a company's direct costs.

You can estimate *marketing costs* by knowing that companies generally spend between 10 percent and 30 percent of their annual costs on marketing. If you know only the marketing budget, or if you know personnel costs, you can estimate the company's annual cost.

For *capital costs*, figure $2,000 to $3,000 per person for computing equipment.

Extended Case Study: Games Software Company

What it does: Develops computer games aimed at girls. Three games are now out.

When and where founded: Founded in the Midwestern U.S. in 1990. At that time, the company made shooter games for boys.

Transformation: In 1996, the company changed its name, moved to Seattle, WA, and changed its focus to software for girls.

Market size: The size of the target market (girls between 11 and 17) is between 7 and 8 million, at least in the U.S. (The company only markets in the U.S.)

New senior management: In 1997, the investors brought in a new chairman and president, both former Microsoft employees.

First product under new structure: The company's first game under the new regime came out in 1998. It was a role-playing adventure game.

Settles on new direction: In 1999, the company licensed a character on which to base future games.

First game based on the character: In 2000, the first new game was released.

Distribution of first game: The first release was distributed through specialty catalogs and the company's Web site. In 2001, Amazon.com and other large online retailers began distributing the game and company sales increased nearly fourfold.

Staffing: In 2000, the company had 10 employees.

Exit strategy: By 2000 management wanted the company to be acquired.

Competition: As of 2000, competing company Mattel's market share of girls' software was 87 percent. That left 13 percent for all the others.

Staffing: By 2001, the company had grown to 14 employees. This tells you that it didn't have a huge investment behind it. If it had, it would have had more than 14 employees by then. It also tells you that it hadn't become very profitable or it would have been sold, as the investors wanted.

Sales: The second game sold better than the first, and the third sold better than either of the other two. The third was ranked number one on Amazon.com.

Growth: The president said in 2001 that the company might expand to 20 employees in 2002. There were two more games in 2001, and the company said it was considering expanding into console games. This means it was doing okay but not fantastic, though there are clear indications of growth and the company is probably working on further investment.

Sales and buzz: In 2001, the company's games were consistently ranked within Amazon's top 25 PC games. This phrasing means they were at the bottom of the 25, or the company would claim to be in the top 10 or top 5. It was doing respectably, especially considering that the overall girls' software market is very small compared to the games market in general.

Licensing: In 2001, the company renewed its license for the character.

Analysis

The company wasn't doing very well in its old location. We know this because:

- When investors bring in new senior management, it is because the company isn't doing well.

- It moved from a smallish non-high-tech city to a larger, more technology-oriented one and changed direction.

Following the move, things improved. We know this because:

- By 1997 it had investors. We know this because of a press release that mentions the investors bringing in new management in 1997. Somewhere along the line the company changed from being an independent startup to a venture-funded company.

- Bringing in two new experienced senior employees implies that the company was getting support from its investors, but it wasn't performing to expectations and wasn't profitable. We can't tell how much cash it had at this point.

We can see the company is doing well. We know this because:

- By 2001, it had three games out and had signed a distribution deal with a successful though small distributor.
- The deal was exclusive, which means that the company was doing all right but not spectacularly. The makers of smash hits don't sign exclusive deals with small publishers. This deal also limits the company's ability to grow, though how much depends on the length of the deal.
- The company still has the same president and CEO. That means the investors are happy with top management. If the investors are happy, the company must be doing well, or at least well enough.
- The licensor has renewed the character license. If the company wasn't doing well, or at least well enough, the licensor would have declined to renew.

Marketing resources are limited. We know this because:

- The company sells through its own Web site.
- If it had more marketing money, it would be working through a bigger distribution channel.

We can infer the following about the company's costs:

- In Seattle, the average salary for a games programmer runs about $100,000, including benefits.
- The company has burned $7 million over five years just on personnel ($100,000 is the average cost; $100,000 x 12 employees [average] = $1.2

million per year. Add 20 percent for overhead = $1.4 million. Times 5 years = $7 million).

- Each game has cost about $1.75 million ($7 million divided by 4 games).

- The company now has low marketing costs, probably about 10 percent of revenues. We believe this is the case because the distributor does the marketing.

- The licensing is probably performance-related because the initial license was for a limited period of time, and the licensor has renewed it. The license probably costs the company 5 to 10 percent of sales.

We can infer that the company is probably breaking even because:

- The company is talking about expanding.

- Two of its three games have been hits.

- New management would probably have been brought in by now, or the company would have folded if it were not performing.

- Revenues from one game per year just about equal the burn rate.

- The company may be turning a profit as its backlist continues to sell.

We can infer the following about revenues:

- Most of the marketing was done through the company's Web site until it got a distribution deal, which gives half of its revenue to the publisher.

- The company's products sell for $20, though the first licensed character game costs $40. We can use an average of $25. It gets $10 of the $25. (Retailers take 45 percent; distributors take 15 percent.)

- The cost of goods is about $2.

- Net per game is $8.

- Therefore, we can guess that at best, the company has sold 875,000 games over five years ($7 million overall revenues divided by $8 net per game), an average of 220,000 games per title.

To check ourselves, here's what we know about the industry:

- Mattel's Barbie games make up 75 percent of the $160 million per year girls' games market. This leaves a maximum of $40 million to be divided among the other players. We're guessing that our company has annual revenues of about $2 million, which gives it a 5 percent market share of that $40 million, but only a 1 percent market share of the girls' games market.

- Purple Moon, which became a subsidiary of Mattel, sold 250,000 copies of a girl's game in 1998. An article in the *Wall Street Journal* calls 250,000 games sold "a definite hit." If our company is selling 220,000 games per title (and it is probably doing more with each new game), each title is a hit.

- The average computer game costs about $1 million to develop. If we're right that our company is spending $1.75 million to develop each game, it is pretty much in line with the average, which means it is working within industry benchmarks.

Appendix

Glossary of Statistics Terms

Adjusted numbers. Raw numbers that have been reworked by the gatherer before release; for example, to account for seasonal variations or changes in the value of the dollar over time.

Analysis. The determination of relationships among data. Analysis makes sense of the data and puts it in some context.

Average. A number that typifies a group of numbers. There are three common types of averages: mean, median, and mode (see below).

Bell curve. A graph in which the values are concentrated at the midpoint and taper out evenly in both directions.

Census. A complete count of a thing or population to be measured.

Continuous data. Data that can be measured using any point along a continuum to describe their values, like weights and heights.

Correlation. A method of data analysis in which the relationship between two measurements is explored.

Derivation. A methodology for producing statistics in which information is extracted or reformatted from raw data. Constructing an index is one form of derivation. Changing units of measurement is another, as when a daily rate is calculated by dividing a yearly rate by 365.

Discrete data. Raw numbers that can only be measured in terms of specific values, such as whole people or whole cars.

Estimate. An approximation of an unknown value based on an extrapolation from a known value. Estimation may be used with current and future measurements.

Experiment. A process of observation or study that results in the collection of data.

Forecasting. A methodology in which known measurements are used to predict the value of unknown measurements that will be discernible at some future time.

Index. One number that summarizes multiple measurements and expresses them in terms of a common base. An index may represent measurements or counts of many things, or different aspects of one thing. One example is the Consumer Price Index.

Interval data. A representation of the difference between two measurements. Interval data are best used when at least one of the measurements is known.

Mean. The arithmetic average in a group of numbers. The mean is derived by adding up all the values and dividing by the number of measurements. The mean may indicate hypothetical rather than real values.

Measurement. The use of instruments or devices to gather data.

Median. The midpoint in a group of numbers; a real or hypothetical value at which half the numbers in the group fall above and half fall below.

Mode. An average that represents the most frequently found numbers in a group. There can be more than one mode in a group. Unlike means and medians, a mode must reflect real values.

Nominal data. A type of statistic that represents categories that are not assigned numerical values.

Observation. A methodology in which the subject is examined in its natural setting.

Panel. An ongoing survey. Panels provide more data than a single survey, and they allow for follow-up over time.

Percentage. An expression of the relationship between a part and the whole that reduces counts to a common scale based on 100.

Percentiles. An indication, based on 100, of how data are distributed. A percentile is a number below which a certain percent of the data fall. For example, the 90th percentile is the number below which 90 percent of the values occur.

Precision. The accuracy of a survey. The precision is proportional to the square root of the sample size.

Probability. An expression of the likelihood that something will occur. Probability is calculated based on the number of times an event occurs when a random experiment is run many times. A low degree of probability indicates less likelihood that the event will occur.

Probable error. Probable error is a measure of how accurate the data are.

Questionnaire. A measurement of attitudes, behavior, or other values that produces a snapshot of them but does not measure against a standard. A questionnaire differs from a test, which does measure against a standard.

Random sample. A methodology of sampling, or taking a representative portion of a group, in which the elements making up the sample are selected by chance. True random samples are so difficult and expensive to obtain that often variations on the random sample are used.

Ranking. A hierarchical comparison. Two kinds of numbers are involved in ranking: the raw data, and the rank or rating number. A searcher might seek the rank number, the raw data, or both.

Rate. A rate is a measure of the change of one thing over time. For example, the rate of inflation expresses the difference between a price index at an earlier time and a later time.

Rating. A subjective measure of something that has been assigned a numerical value. Scales such as "agree strongly," "agree," "agree somewhat," "disagree somewhat, "disagree," and "strongly disagree" are examples of ratings. When the values have been converted to numbers, these types of data are also called ordinal data because they define relative positions in a series.

Ratio. One number divided by another.

Raw numbers. Pure data. A type of statistic that represents counts or measures.

Sample. A representative "taste" of a group. Samples may be used when a census is too expensive or impossible to implement.

Significance. A measure of correlation; that is, whether one thing is related to another thing.

Standard deviation. When considering averages, watch for the term "standard deviation." Standard deviation is a measure of distribution or variation of numbers. The smaller the standard deviation, the closer together the numbers. The larger, the farther apart.

Standard error. A measure of how accurate the data are.

Test. A measurement of the way something or someone performs compared to a standard. A test differs from a questionnaire in that the questionnaire does not measure against a standard.

Validity. Truth or accuracy in statistical data and its representation. Degree of validity is affected by the method for gathering, manipulating, and interpreting the data.

About the Author

Paula Berinstein is a late but enthusiastic bloomer when it comes to a career in business. Running her own research firm after having spent eight years as a programmer and systems analyst at Rocketdyne, she learned the hard way what it takes to succeed in business: carefully defining and wooing a receptive, reachable market. Ms. Berinstein is one of the few people on Earth who enjoys writing business plans. She is currently co-founder and Executive Vice President, Product Strategy for Paula Hollywood, Inc., an eponymous software company that makes easy-to-use 3D character animation products for the masses.

Index

More Great Books from Information Today, Inc.

The Skeptical Business Searcher
The Information Advisor's Guide to Evaluating Web Data, Sites, and Sources

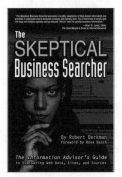

By Robert Berkman • Foreword by Reva Basch

This is the experts' guide to finding high-quality company and industry data on the free Web. Information guru Robert Berkman offers business Internet users effective strategies for identifying and evaluating no-cost online information sources, emphasizing easy-to-use techniques for recognizing bias and misinformation. You'll learn where to go for company backgrounders, sales and earnings data, SEC filings and stockholder reports, public records, market research, competitive intelligence, staff directories, executive biographies, survey/poll data, news stories, and hard-to-find information about small businesses and niche markets. The author's unique table of "Internet Information Credibility Indicators" allows readers to systematically evaluate Web site reliability. Supported by a Web page.

2003/softbound/ISBN 0-910965-66-8 • $29.95

International Business Information on the Web
Searcher Magazine's Guide to Sites and Strategies for Global Business Research

By Sheri R. Lanza • Edited by Barbara Quint

Here is the first ready-reference for effective worldwide business research, written by experienced international business researcher Sheri R. Lanza and edited by *Searcher* magazine's Barbara Quint. This book helps readers identify overseas buyers, find foreign suppliers, investigate potential partners and competitors, uncover international market research and industry analysis, and much more. As a reader bonus, a companion Web directory features links to more than 1,000 top sites for global business research.

2001/380 pp/softbound/ISBN 0-910965-46-3 • $29.95

Super Searchers Cover the World
The Online Secrets of International Business Researchers

By Mary Ellen Bates • Edited by Reva Basch
Foreword by Clare Hart

The Internet has made it possible for more businesses to think internationally, and to take advantage of the expanding global economy. Through 15 interviews with leading online searchers, Mary Ellen Bates explores the challenges of reaching outside a researcher's geographic area to do effective international business research. Experts from around the world—librarians and researchers from government organizations, multinational companies, universities, and small businesses—discuss such issues as nonnative language sources, cultural biases, and the reliability of information. Supported by the Super Searchers Web page.

2001/250 pp/softbound/ISBN 0-910965-54-4 • $24.95

Building and Running a Successful Research Business
A Guide for the Independent Information Professional

By Mary Ellen Bates • Edited by Reva Basch

This is the handbook every aspiring independent information professional needs to launch, manage, and build a research business. Organized into four sections, "Getting Started," "Running the Business," "Marketing," and "Researching," the book walks you through every step of the process. Author and long-time independent researcher Mary Ellen Bates covers everything from "is this right for you?" to closing the sale, managing clients, promoting your business, and tapping into powerful information sources.

2003/360 pp/softbound/ISBN 0-910965-62-5 • $29.95

Super Searchers Make It on Their Own
Top Independent Information Professionals Share Their
Secrets for Starting and Running a Research Business

By Suzanne Sabroski • Edited by Reva Basch

If you want to start and run a successful Information Age business, read this book. Here, for the first time anywhere, 11 of the world's top research entrepreneurs share their strategies for starting a business, developing a niche, finding clients, doing the research, networking with peers, and staying up-to-date with Web resources and technologies. You'll learn how these super searchers use the Internet to find, organize, analyze, and package information for their clients. Most importantly, you'll discover their secrets for building a profitable research business.

2002/336 pp/softbound/ISBN 0-910965-59-5 • $24.95

Internet Prophets
Enlightened E-Business Strategies for Every Budget

By Mary Diffley

Since the bursting of the dot.com balloon, companies are approaching e-business with a new wariness—and rightly so, according to author and entrepreneur Mary Diffley. In *Internet Prophets*, Diffley speaks directly to the skeptics, serving up straightforward advice that will help even the most technophobic executive do more business on the Web. This readable, easy-to-use handbook is the first to detail the costs of proven e-commerce strategies, matching successful techniques with budgetary considerations for companies of all types and sizes. Unlike other books, *Internet Prophets* gets down to the nitty-gritty that every businessperson wants to know: "What's it going to cost?"

2002/366 pp/softbound/ISBN 0-910965-55-2 • $29.95

The Extreme Searcher's Guide to Web Search Engines
A Handbook for the Serious Searcher, 2nd Edition

By Randolph Hock • Foreword by Reva Basch

"Whatever your Internet search needs, the second edition of Hock's book is essential reading." —CHOICE

In this completely revised and expanded version of his award-winning book, the "extreme searcher," Randolph (Ran) Hock, digs even deeper, covering all the most popular Web search tools, plus a half-dozen of the newest and most exciting search engines to come down the pike. This is a practical, user-friendly guide supported by a regularly updated Web site.

2001/250 pp/softbound/ISBN 0-910965-47-1 • $24.95

Naked in Cyberspace
How to Find Personal Information Online, 2nd Edition

By Carole A. Lane • Foreword by Beth Givens

In this fully revised and updated second edition of her bestselling guide, author Carole A. Lane surveys the types of personal records that are available on the Internet and online services. Lane explains how researchers find and use personal data, identifies the most useful sources of information about people, and offers advice for readers with privacy concerns. You'll learn how to use online tools and databases to gain competitive intelligence, locate and investigate people, access public records, identify experts, find new customers, recruit employees, search for assets, uncover criminal records, conduct genealogical research, and much more. Supported by a Web page.

2002/586 pp/softbound/ISBN 0-910965-50-1 • $29.95

Web of Deception
Misinformation on the Internet

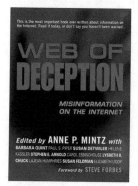

Edited by Anne P. Mintz • Foreword by Steve Forbes

Intentionally misleading or erroneous information on the Web can wreak havoc on your health, privacy, investments, business decisions, online purchases, legal affairs, and more. Until now, the breadth and significance of this growing problem for Internet users had yet to be fully explored. In *Web of Deception*, Anne P. Mintz (Director of Knowledge Management at Forbes, Inc.) brings together 10 information industry gurus to illuminate the issues and help you recognize and deal with the flood of deception and misinformation in a range of critical subject areas. A must-read for any Internet searcher who needs to evaluate online information sources and avoid Web traps.

2002/278 pp/softbound/ISBN 0-910965-60-9 • $24.95

The Librarian's Internet Survival Guide
Strategies for the High-Tech Reference Desk

By Irene E. McDermott • Edited by Barbara Quint

In this authoritative and tremendously useful guide, Irene McDermott helps her fellow reference librarians succeed in the bold new world of the Web. *The Survival Guide* provides easy access to the information librarians need when the pressure is on: trouble-shooting tips and advice, Web resources for answering reference questions, and strategies for managing information and keeping current. In addition to helping librarians make the most of Web tools and resources, McDermott covers a full range of important issues including Internet training, privacy, child safety, helping patrons with special needs, building library Web pages, and much more.

2002/296 pp/softbound/ISBN 1-57387-129-X • $29.50

The Accidental Webmaster

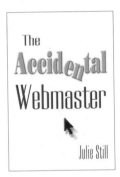

By Julie Still

Here is a lifeline for the individual who has not been trained as a Webmaster, but who—whether by choice or under duress—has become one nonetheless. While most Webmastering books focus on programming and related technical issues, *The Accidental Webmaster* helps readers deal with the full range of challenges they face on the job. Author, librarian, and accidental Webmaster Julie Still offers advice on getting started, setting policies, working with ISPs, designing home pages, selecting content, drawing site traffic, gaining user feedback, fundraising, avoiding copyright problems, and much more.

2003/205 pp/softbound/ISBN 1-57387-164-8 • $29.50

Smart Services
Competitive Information Strategies, Solutions, and Success Stories for Service Businesses

By Deborah C. Sawyer

Here is the first book to focus specifically on the competitive information needs of service-oriented firms. Author, entrepreneur, and business consultant Deborah C. Sawyer illuminates the many forms of competition in service businesses, identifies the most effective information resources for competitive intelligence (CI), and provides a practical framework for identifying and studying competitors in order to gain a competitive advantage. *Smart Services* is a roadmap for every service company owner, manager, or executive who expects to compete effectively in the Information Age.

2002/256 pp/softbound/ISBN 0-910965-56-0 • $29.95

Ask for these books at your local bookstore or order online at www.infotoday.com

For a complete catalog, contact:

Information Today, Inc.
143 Old Marlton Pike
Medford, NJ 08055
800/300-9868 • 609/654-6266 • e-mail: custserv@infotoday.com